MIRRORS OF MOSCOW

MIRRORS OF MOSCOW

BY

LOUISE BRYANT

With five illustrations by
CÉSARE

HYPERION PRESS, INC.
WESTPORT, CONNECTICUT

Library of Congress Cataloging in Publication Data

Bryant, Louise, 1890-1936.
  Mirrors of Moscow.

    Reprint of the ed. published by T. Seltzer, New
York.
    1. Russia--Biography. 2. Russia--History--
Revolution, 1917-1921. I. Title.
DK253.B7 1973   947.084'1'0922   73-834
ISBN 0-88355-030-X

Published in 1923
by Thomas Seltzer, Inc., New York.
Copyright 1923
by Thomas Seltzer, Inc.

First Hyperion reprint edition 1973

Library of Congress Catalogue Number 73-834

ISBN 0-88355-030-X

Printed in the United States of America

TO THREE WISE EDITORS—

M. KOENIGSBERG
BRADFORD MERRILL
PHILLIP FRANCIS

CONTENTS

ILLUSTRATIONS

FOREWORD

Revolution! The air is filled with flames and fumes. The shapes of men, seen through the smoke, become distorted and unreal. Promethean supermen, they seem, giants in sin or virtue, Satans or saviours. But, in truth, behind the screen of smoke and flame they are like other men: no larger and no smaller, no better and no worse: all creatures of the same incessant passions, hungers, vanities and fears.

So it is in Russia. And in this book I have tried to show the leaders of the revolution as they really are, as I know them in their homes, where the red glare does not penetrate and they live as other men.

Great events make great men. For to be strong enough even to maintain one's self amid great events is to be great. Without the event the strength is nothing. Had the revolt of 1917 failed, like the revolt of 1905, Lenin would have worked his life out in an attic in Geneva, Trotsky would have lived and died in a New York garret, Kalinin would have remained a disappointed, debt-burdened peasant, Tchicherin a futile ex-diplomatist in exile. The world would not have known their names: just as the world would not have known Napoleon or Danton or Marat or Robespierre had Louis XVI been a trifle less desperately dull. But the revolt of 1917 became a revolution and its colossal drive and heave flung up the exiles to greatness. As men it did not change them.

They differ from the political leaders one meets in Washington, London and Paris, largely because they are able to be franker and more themselves. Public opinion, which is the boon of politicians and the bane of statesmen, does not drive them to drab conformity or high-sounding platitude. The public they have to satisfy is small and sophisticated—the trade unions of the larger cities. And these workingmen demand, above all else, frankness and the unpowdered truth. An address by Lenin is, therefore, as direct, unsentimental and full of facts as a statement to a board of directors by an executive of an American corporation. The slow, strong wants of the peasants have to be heeded, too; but they are simple wants, land and free trade, and do not yet touch intricate things, remote from the daily life of the farm, like

FOREWORD

foreign affairs and higher economics. In the end the peasants will rule Russia, but to-day public opinion is the opinion of the class-conscious workingmen of the cities. Therefore, the leaders of Russia can afford to be frank.

In the western democracies, politics is the art of seeming frank while not being so. Only three types of politicians ever emerge in the highest places. First, the statesman of brilliant intellectual understanding, like Lloyd George, who always knows what he ought to do, and never does it—until the public also comes to understand, usually some months, or years, later. Second, the sentimentalist, who is always able to muddle an inconvenient understanding of facts and muffle his conscience with high-sounding principles that endear him to the public heart. Third, the kindly blockhead, who discovers what ought to be done just a little later than the public. These types do not exist in Russia. The trade unions compel the Russian politician to be a stark realist, talking frankly, acting on the best information he can obtain and giving that information fully to his public. The leaders pictured in this book will seem, therefore, franker and more direct than the leaders of the western world.

They will also seem more desperate; not because
it is their natural character to be desperate but
because they face as desperate a problem as ever
strained the human brain. They have been caught,
from the first, on the horns of the revolutionary
dilemma. The same intolerable breakdown of
economic life, which alone makes revolution possible, also predestines revolution to almost certain failure. That dull beast, the public, will
move to revolution only when life has become
unbearable, only when the established order has
broken down so completely that ruins alone remain. Revolution does not come before ruin.
And to build on ruins a new and fairer life is
a task almost beyond the powers of men. So
much of the exhausted energy of the nation must
be consumed in re-establishing the mere funda-
mentals of life—food, shelter, clothing and se-
curity from fear—that little remains to attack the
task of remoulding life in a shape that is closer
to the heart's desire. But to this task the leaders
of Russia have dedicated their lives. And if they
succeed or if they fail, they will be remembered
always for their courage in following an ideal
through destruction, famine, death and the hatred
of the world.

FOREWORD

Here, then, they are: the Russians of to-day: close to the Tartar and the Cossack of the plain, children of serfs and Norsemen and Mongols—close to the earth and striving for the stars.

Louise Bryant.

LENIN AND HIS SUBORDINATES

NIKOLAI LENIN

CHRISTIAN RAKOVSKY

ABRAHAM KRASNICHAKOV

LEO KAMINEV AND GREGORY ZINOVIEV

PETER STOOTCHKA

ALIEXIEV IVANOVITCH RYKOV

LENIN

LENIN AND HIS SUBORDINATES

NIKOLAI LENIN

LENIN became an active revolutionist through the spiritual motives that have moved all great reformers—not because he himself was hungry and an outcast, but because he could not stand by unmoved in a world where other men were hungry and outcast. Such characters are predestined internationalists; the very quality that lifts them above materialism places them above borders and points of geography; they strive for the universal good. Lenin believes that the only thing worth living for is the next generation. Communism is his formula for saving the next generation from the injustices and inequalities of the present.

When I think of Lenin and his place in the Russian revolution I am reminded of a statue which, until the late Fall of the year 1918, adorned the busy square before the entrance to the Nikoliavski station in Petrograd. It represented one of the former rulers of Russia astride a huge stallion. One could not fail to be struck by the tremendous strength of the animal and the frailty of the rider.

3

The contrast was intentional; the titled sculptor meant to warn his sovereign of the dangers threatening the throne. Russia was the wild horse, fierce, untamed, powerful, a force as yet unaroused but which might wake up any moment and cast off its royal burden.

When Lenin took the reins of state, he was in exactly the same position as a man riding a runaway horse. The utmost his constituents could have expected was that he would guide Russia away from complete destruction. They could hold him responsible for immediate situations but not for ultimate results. To what goal those vast urges and desires which caused the revolution would carry Russia, was beyond him or any man to command. His heart and his mind wished to direct it toward the crimson portals of socialism. Russia, however, in its stampede seems to have slowed up dangerously near the old, familiar gates of capitalism. Nevertheless, she will never be the same; Lenin is responsible for it that Russia has forever gained the larger fruits of the revolution.

Legends spring up around every famous man, manufactured largely by his enemies, who spread tales of his lavish extravagance, his vices, his affairs with women. It is important to know such

4

facts about a man's life. His personal relationships mean a great deal; if he fails in these, he eventually fails in all ways. The life of the leader of a great world movement must harmonize with his doctrines; his conduct must be as austere or as lax as his doctrines dictate. That is why we have a natural antipathy to dissolute priests and none at all to dissolute poets and Bacchanalians. So it is worthy of note that even the narrowest moralist could not pick a flaw in Lenin's personal conduct. I am convinced that if he had lived in any other way than he has, he could not have maintained his remarkable poise.

Whatever inward storms arose he was impressive because of his outward serenity, because of his calm, majestic as a Chinese Buddha's. Without any fuss he took power, faced world opposition, civil war, disease, defeat and even success. Without fuss he retired for a space, and without fuss he has returned again. His quiet authoritativeness inspired more confidence than could any amount of pomp. I know of no character in history capable, as he was through such distressing days, of such complete, aristocratic composure.

Every normal man is pushed forward or back to some degree by women. It is my theory that Lenin's amazing stability was substantially strengthened by the women who meant most to him. Those women were: his mother, his wife, his sister and his lifelong friend and, in late years, chief secretary, Fotiva.

During all the years since the Bolshevik uprising, Fotiva has been his assistant. On days when he was ill or away in the country she actually had charge of the office. She is a highly efficient woman of forty, tall, dark, healthy and full of enthusiasm. She is quiet, also, and cheerful, and creates a pleasant atmosphere about her.

Lenin's office, with Fotiva managing all the under-secretaries, is an agreeable office to enter. You never feel like an intruder, nor, at the same time, that it is a place to loaf in, which means that she knows how to preserve a happy balance. In all one's dealings with Fotiva, one finds her a woman of her word. She has the very un-Russian quality of always being on time for appointments and never going back on her promises. She is a Communist of old standing and occasionally contributes articles to newspapers and magazines.

As for Madame Lenin, no one could be disturbed in her presence. How different the state of the Soviet Premier's temper might have been on occasions were his wife the sort of woman who would weep because her apartment in the Kremlin was small, or would quarrel with the other Commissars' wives, or would be jealous of Fotiva. The truth is, she admires Fotiva and is entirely glad of her existence.

Madame Lenin, whose real name is Nadezhda Konstantinova Krupskaya Ulianova, acted for many years as Lenin's secretary. Only ill health prevented her from continuing the work.

When Lenin was editor of Iskra in Switzerland, she was the secretary of the whole Iskra organization, which not only had charge of publishing a newspaper but carried on vast party activities. All the correspondence was in her hands. At one time she was in communication with every revolutionist in Russia.

That is one reason why she is so well known from one end of the country to the other and why people still continue to call her by her revolutionary name.

Under the Tsar, Lenin was twice exiled and Krupskaya always shared his fate. Together they passed hard years in Switzerland, England and especially Paris, where for two years Lenin spent almost his entire time studying in the national library. His only means of existence was by his writings, and he wrote solely for and about the revolution—by no means a remunerative occupation. The entire period of exile extended over ten long years. In that time the Lenins never knew a day of ease or luxury. They had become accustomed to privations long before the revolution, had lived in the meanest quarters of every city they visited, occupying, as a rule, only one room, where they ate, slept, studied and carried on their revolutionary work.

It does not seem mere romance to infer that Krupskaya has had a good deal to do with keeping Lenin's nerves steady.

There were moments when Trotsky lost his head, when the Extraordinary Commission gave way to doubts, when Tchicherin hesitated—but never Lenin. Without doubt the secret of his power is that he is the only man in Russia, of any political group, whose purpose always remained clear and whose hand never trembled.

He made all manner of blunders. That he was able to admit his mistakes emphasizes his quality of mind. It is a scientific mind: a mind so well disciplined that he is able to face every fact, failure as well as success. Moreover, he has a way of

8

grasping a situation almost by instinct; at least he grasps it at a stroke.

Nikolai Lenin strives for two great things—to westernize Russia and to keep alive the fountainhead of the Socialist State.

He told me that he did not want to grant a single foreign concession, whether a factory, a mine or a forest concession, unless he could establish a similar Russian institution alongside of it so that the Russians might continually see before their eyes the superiority of the American or the English way of doing things.

He is more interested in America than in any other country.

I remember one afternoon just before I went up to interview him, an official in the Foreign Office told me that if America did not hurry and start trade negotiations with Russia, Russia would be forced to make a trade alliance with Japan. I mentioned this to Lenin and he said:

"Nonsense! Even if we could trust Japan, which we cannot, what could she give us? We need thousands of tractors, railway engines, cars, things like that. We must get such things from America, we must make friends with America."

I think he feels in closer contact with the United

States, too, because of the number of former exiles who once fled to our shores and who returned after the revolution and now hold office under the Soviet Government. He likes the way they have been trained here.

It has given him the idea of working concessions in the manner I have described. He also feels gratitude toward Raymond Robins and always asks about him, considers William C. Bullitt a man of honor, while John Reed was as near to his heart as was ever any Russian.

He is continually reading American papers, books and magazines. When I came home I sent him the "Mirrors of Washington," and I know how he will chuckle over it as he used to chuckle over William Hard's articles in the *New Republic*.

He admires American energy so much that he comes very near understanding an American reporter's need for on-the-minute news, which no other Soviet official appreciates, except Trotsky.

I will never forget the day during the blackest time of the blockade when I went to Lenin and asked permission to go to the Middle East after the Foreign Office had flatly refused me this permission. He simply looked up from his work and smiled.

"I am glad to see there is someone in Russia," he said, "with enough energy to go exploring. You might get killed down there, but you will have the most remarkable experience of your life; it is worth taking chances for."

In two days I was on my way, with every necessary *probsk* to ride on any train or stop in any government hotel. I carried a personal letter from Lenin and had two soldiers for escort! Any other official in Russia would have considered me an infernal nuisance even to suggest such an adventure in the middle of a revolution.

Lenin has always stood for allowing political enemies to leave Russia. This shows an unexpected softness in his make-up which only those who know him well comprehend.

Naturally, the Cheka disagrees with him on this point, holding that when these people "succeed in getting out of Russia" they are just as much a part of the war on Russia as the White Army is.

The explanation is that Lenin has by no means a forbidding personality: revenge never occupies his mind. He will flay an opponent in a debate and walk out of the hall arm-in-arm with him.

He is extraordinarily human and good-natured and wishes to see everyone happy.

In the beginning of the revolution he imagined that he could maintain a free press, free speech and be liberal toward his enemies. But he found himself faced by a situation where iron discipline was the only method capable of saving the day.

There were times when he rather ruthlessly suppressed the Anarchists, but only because they threatened violence at every step. The supreme test of his power to forgive came during the Social Revolutionary trial, which took place in the summer of this year. He was lying ill in the country from the effects of an operation to remove an assassin's bullet from his neck. The people responsible for the bullet were duly sentenced to death after a long and illuminating trial, in which the absolute evidence of their guilt was established. It was through the irrepressible influence of Lenin that their sentences were all commuted.

Lenin never scorns a deep affection or a personal sentiment. At the time of Kropotkin's death, the widow and daughter sent a telegram to Lenin asking that the Anarchist leaders then imprisoned in Moscow be allowed to attend the funeral. Lenin let them go "on their honor" without guards for three days.

The Cheka objected, the Foreign Office objected and the Moscow Soviet objected, but Lenin's will, as usual, prevailed. This generosity toward his enemies costs Lenin nothing and helps him to maintain his astonishing equilibrium.

Every man in Lenin's cabinet, with the exception of Trotsky and Tchicherin, has been working with him for over twenty years; they really are his disciples. He knows their characteristics as well as if they were his own children. He knows just how much brains and ability each one has.

Once he was asked why he keeps a certain man, who is so obviously inferior to the others. He smiled and said, "Isn't it always necessary to have at least one fool in every cabinet?"

Lenin makes an interesting contrast to Woodrow Wilson. Lenin picks the strongest minds he can get and complains that he cannot find enough brains. He feels a particular lack of brains in the diplomatic service. The small corps around Tchicherin will be highly inadequate to spread over the earth when the time comes for sending ambassadors and consuls to every country in the world. Russia will be as slip-shoddily represented as America. It is only the English who realize the value of a school for diplomats.

Lenin has never been known to dismiss a man after he has worked with him only half a year. And no man has ever deserted him no matter how Lenin may have ridden down his opposition.

Politically, Lenin has a hard, cold, calculating brain and uses all men to his own ends. They forgive him because he does it openly and for no personal gain.

The Soviet Premier is by no means a vain man. He rarely autographs pictures of himself, and the diary the American editors always request us to ask him about will never be written. He says he is too tired to write down notes after the day's mass of work has been done. Lack of vanity and conceit is an equal reason.

He hates to be flattered or to have his portrait painted. He was in real distress because he consented to allow Claire Sheridan to do his bust. Angelica Balabonova was spending an evening with the Lenins in their apartment that same week and she said, reprovingly:

"Revolutionaries have something else to do beside spend their time in such a way."

Lenin answered:

"I agree with you and I felt unhappy about it, but when Comrade Litvinov asked me to sit, it seemed such a small matter that I didn't like to be disagreeable."

As a matter of fact, he only gave Mrs. Sheridan a few hours and, from her own account, worked all the time he was posing.

In private conversation, no subject is too small for his attention. I remember one time some foreign delegates were talking about the Russian theatre and particularly about the lack of costumes and stage property.

Someone said that Gellser, the great ballerina, complained that she had no silk stockings. The delegates were of the opinion that this was a slight matter. Not so Lenin.

He frowned and said he would see to it that Gellser had everything she needed immediately. Calling his stenographer, he dictated a letter to Lunacharsky about it. Yet Lenin had never seen Gellser dance and took no further interest in the affair.

On the one occasion, in three years, that he found time to attend the theatre, he chose Shakespeare. Telephoning to Lunacharsky he announced, "I want to see the best performance at the Art Theatre."

Lunacharsky was in doubt but mentioned Helena Soochachova's superb performance in "Twelfth Night." Lenin interrupted, "I'll see that." And once in the theatre he forgot his million worries and enjoyed himself with the abandon of a child. Hunting and horseback riding he goes in for with the same enthusiasm.

I have often been asked just what was back of Lenin and his colleagues; what moved them to attempt to establish Socialism at such a moment and against such odds.

Most of us agree that it was partly a revolt against an age of commercialism. But fundamentally it was a demonstration.

Radek told Arthur Ransome that the Bolshevik leaders did not expect to hold power two months when they seized the reins of government.

Half a year after Lenin became Premier, he wrote:

"If they crush us now, they can never efface the fact that we have been. The idea will go on."

It is ridiculous to contend that Lenin has "repented" because he has found it necessary to go back to a modified capitalism. One need not repent because one has failed. If Lenin is forced to abandon every vestige of Communism, it will not mean that he no longer believes in Marx.

It will more likely mean that, finding circumstances too much for him, he is retreating to a position as strategic as he can find. That he remains master of the retreat indicates that he will move backward only as far as he is pushed.

It is hard now to realize on what a fine thread many important situations during the last years have hung, situations that would have completely changed future history. It is hard to realize, for example, that the Germans almost reached Paris or that the White forces almost took Petrograd.

Perhaps Lenin was the only man in Russia who fully realized how near the Soviets came to being overthrown. There was one moment when the morale of the Red Army was exceedingly low and when even the trusted Lettish sharpshooters guarding the Kremlin grew discouraged and sampled the wine in the Kremlin cellars to make life more interesting. A Lett who went through these days told me an amazing story.

"One night the Old Man himself came down to the barracks, called the officers out, felt in our pockets and, finding one or two flasks of vodka, smashed them on the cobblestones and went away without saying a word. He only had to come once; we were deeply ashamed."

How much truth there is in this story I do not know, but it sounds so exactly like Lenin that I am inclined to give it full credence.

From this low ebb he built his power solidly, never forgetting to reckon on the peasants. Now face to face at last with Mr. Lloyd George, Lenin is backed by a strong Red Army and a loyal staff.

From the moment he took office Lenin never had a serious political rival. And the blockade bestowed on him a peculiar legendary significance which will remain with him as long as he does not leave Russia.

Nikolai Lenin has been a conscious revolutionist since he was sixteen, but he has never been a "terrorist." A terrorist, in revolutionary vernacular, is one who believes in individual acts of violence. His mind is too ordered and his plans too wide for such incoherent emotionalism.

His father was a small landed (hereditary) noble, holding the office of State Councillor, having an estate in Simbirsk. Vladimir Illyitch Ulianov, which is Lenin's real name, was born there on April 10, 1870. There were in all five children, three boys and two girls.

It was a closely-knit family. One of Lenin's best friends and advisers even now is his sister Anna. She spends most of her time in Moscow. He has a brother living in the provinces, who comes to see him occasionally, a quiet, studious man, not interested in politics, and, perhaps, even a little repelled by the strenuousness of them, especially in Russia.

There is no doubt that Lenin's determination to fight the Tsar's government crystallized at the time of his brother's death. His eldest brother, Alexander, was away at the University of Petrograd. All that they heard from him at home was about the winning of gold medals and honors of all sorts until one day came the terrible news that he had been arrested for a plot against the Czar.

Lenin's mother, Maria Alexandrovna, rushed away to Petrograd. When she reached her son's side he burst into tears and immediately confessed everything to her. He begged her to forgive him for bringing sorrow to his beloved family. At the trial he made no defense and asked no mercy. He was executed in the courtyard of Schlüsselberg fortress on May 20, 1886.

And back home in the little preparatory school called the "gymnasium" were two youths profoundly touched by this tragedy. One was the present Premier and the other was Alexander Kerensky, whose father was master of the school; evolution works in strange ways.

The Lenins have no children. They have devoted their lives to the revolution. Madame Lenin is a pale, scholarly woman, usually in very poor health. It was she who devised the new scheme for adult education in Russia which Lunacharsky told me has proved highly efficient.

Lenin adores his wife and speaks of her with enthusiasm. The first time I told him that I wanted to meet her, he said:

"Yes, you must do that because you will like her, she is so intelligent."

I found her both intelligent and sympathetic.

She invited me to take tea with her in her apartment and I was very glad to go, since I wanted to see for myself how the Lenins lived.

They have two small rooms, which is the regulation in overcrowded Moscow. Everything was spotlessly clean, though, as she explained, she had no servant. There were quantities of books, plants in the windows, a few chairs, a table, beds and no pictures on the walls.

I found her to have the same charm which Lenin has and the same way of focusing all her attention on what her visitor is saying.

When you go to Lenin's office he always jumps up and comes forward smiling, shakes hands warmly and pushes forward a comfortable chair. When you are seated he draws up another chair, leans forward and begins to talk as if there was nothing else to do in the world but visit.

He likes harmless gossip and will laugh mightily over some story about how Mr. Vanderlip fought with a Hungarian over a few sticks of wood on a cold day, or an incident which occurred on a train, or in the street. He himself loves to tell stories, and tells them very well. But no conversation runs on lightly for long with Lenin. He will stop suddenly in his laughter and say:

"What sort of a man is Mr. Harding, and what is his background?"

It does not matter how determined one is to ply him with questions, one always goes away astonished because one has talked so much and answered so many questions instead of asking them. He has an extraordinary way of drawing one out and of putting one in an expansive mood.

This capacity for personal contact must be a big influence with the men with whom he comes constantly in touch.

No wonder he dominates his Cabinet! When he narrows his small Tartar eyes, looks at one with such understanding and intimacy, one feels he is the best friend in the world; it would be impossible to oppose him.

We are wont to think of Lenin as a destroyer, but he is more of a builder.

When he could not build a Communist State he did not throw up his hands. He built the best State he could in its place and now he is saying that Russia is the safest country in Europe; that it has reached its lowest level and is climbing up, while other countries in Europe are still declining.

It is just possible that he is right!

CHRISTIAN RAKOVSKY

THE world, which now very generally concedes to Lenin great political adroitness, is not fully aware of the extent of his talent. What other man could have managed, under the stress of the hour, to have kept control of the politics of great Russia, the Ukraine, the Far Eastern Republic and even of China? And not only does he guide the destinies of these Republics, he subordinates the men at the head of them. Thus he is consolidating Russia. In Moscow, people believe that Lenin will some day bring the Baltic States back into the Soviet federation.

Christian Rakovsky, President of the Ukraine, never reaches any important decision without consulting Lenin. Rakovsky is an interesting personality and a man whose star is ascending. He is undoubtedly one of the strongest men in Russia, and since Lenin backs him, he ought to go far.

Rakovsky was born in the little Bulgarian town of Kotel. His family is one of the best known in all the Balkans. The name Rakovsky is woven through Balkan history and revolutionary struggles.

Expelled from college for revolutionary activities, young Rakovsky went to Geneva in 1890 and joined the Russian Social Democratic Party. In 1892 he was arrested in Geneva for an encounter with an agent-provocateur; he was expelled from Berlin the same year for participation in the German labor movement.

After some difficulty he was permitted to remain in France, where he carried on his studies. He was graduated from a French medical college in 1897 and returned to Bulgaria.

Two years later he published a large historical volume called "Russian Policy in the East." He also wrote what was considered a brilliant dissertation on criminology and degeneracy.

Rakovsky went to Russia in 1900, but was immediately arrested and expelled by the Tsar's police. He returned to Germany and there he wrote his best known book, "Present Day France," which was published under the pen-name of Insarov.

A short time after completing this book he entered the judicial faculty of the University of Paris, but was so interested in the Russian revolu-

tion that he gave up his post after a year and went
again to Russia, only to be expelled promptly.

He organized the Socialist Party in Roumania
in 1904 and in 1907 was arrested following some
peasant uprising. He was deprived of all political
rights, exiled and forbidden ever to return to
Roumania. But he had such a large and staunch
following and so many serious riots took place that
the Government was too embarrassed to carry out
its decision. In a riot in Bucharest more than fifty
persons were killed. In 1912 he was re-enfran-
chised, which was considered a great victory for
the Roumanian labor leader.

Rakovsky is an habitual publicist; in the course
of his career he has founded ten newspapers.

During the war he was so active in his anti-war
propaganda that he was imprisoned in Roumania,
but the first days of the 1917 revolution gave him
back his freedom when the Russian garrison in
Jassy decided of its own initiative to release all
political prisoners.

He was not popular with the Provisional
Government and, fearing his influence, Burstev
requested his arrest in a note to Tereschendo and
in a telegram to Kerensky. Learning of this order,

he went to Sweden and was in Stockholm at the time of the Bolshevik *coup d'état.*

In 1919 he was elected head of the Ukraine by the action of the Third Congress of Ukrainian Soviets. I say "head" because he is at present Premier, President and Minister of Foreign Affairs as well as a member of the Executive Committee of the Third International in Moscow.

While I was in Moscow Rakovsky and his wife spent several weeks in the house in which I lived. Madame Rakovsky is the sort of woman who adds interesting and insuppressible variety to the leveling influence of the revolution. She is a princess, speaks French in preference to Russian after the manner of the old Russian aristocracy, and still uses a lorgnette. She is an enthusiastic Communist. Everything about her is charming, distinguished and—eminently exclusive! She always accompanies her husband wherever he goes, is present at all interviews, and one can tell by the way he listens to her opinions that he places particular value on her advice.

Rakovsky himself is in manner and appearance more like an Old World diplomat than a revolutionist. But in spite of his suavity he has Lenin's ability to face situations squarely. He once gave me such a frank statement about conditions in the Ukraine that instead of going over the cables to my paper it was officially chucked into the waste basket by Tchicherin.

ABRAHAM KRASNICHAKOV

OUT in Chicago Abraham Moiseyevitch Krasnichakov was plain Mr. Tobinson, but for three years he has enjoyed great authority under his own name as head of the Far Eastern Republic.

There is nothing lacking in either romance or adventure in the story of A. Stroller Tobinson. He was born in the city of Chernobyl, in the province of Kiev, in Russia, and fled to the United States about the time his brother was executed in Odessa for some connection with revolutionary activities. This was in 1904.

Tobinson was a Russian law student of unusual ability, but when he arrived in America a poor immigrant he found his Russian education of little use; he first had to learn the English language.

In Chicago he went to work as a house painter and attended night school. In 1912 he was admitted to the bar, but never was a great success as a lawyer. And while he took only a passive interest in the radical movement, yet he continually gave his services in all sorts of labor cases.

KRASNICHAKOV

Not until he, somehow, became interested in organizing a preparatory school for workers who wanted to go to college did he seem to hit his medium. From that time on he rapidly developed into an organizer and leader, and soon assumed charge of all the educational work connected with the Workers' Institute.

He started with a broad program which shut out all petty, political and group influences. He was a born teacher, and nothing is more rare than a good teacher.

His intense interest in the education of the masses was really what carried him back to Siberia in 1917. And there one of those curious historical situations arose which suddenly thrust him unexpectedly and unprepared into power.

He was one of the numerous candidates for President up before the Constitutional Assembly of the Far Eastern Republic. He certainly never expected to be elected. It was the stupidity of his political rivals which gave him this position.

A day or two before the election some one wrote a vicious attack upon him in one of the papers, asking the people of Siberia if they wanted a "porter," a common house painter, to guide the affairs of the republic.

When Tobinson read this he was furious to think that his hard struggles in America as an emigrant were thrown at him as if they were a disgrace. He sat down and wrote a letter explaining that he had had a good education, both in Russia and America, that he was not actually a workman, but a lawyer. When he had finished writing this explanation, he put it in his pocket and started toward the office of the same paper. On the street he was met by a delegation of workingmen, who threw their arms around him and called him "Comrade."

One of them said: "We were against you until we read what the bourgeois are saying, but now we are all on your side; we want a man who is one of us." This was the beginning of Tobinson's popularity and this is the story of how he became President of the Far Eastern Republic.

Tobinson was not a Communist. His connections had been more with groups who simply revolted against the medieval tyranny which had existed in Russia. But he admired Lenin above all the revolutionists, and was of the opinion that Lenin was the only revolutionary leader who could hold Russia together. Therefore he secretly allied himself with the Communist government at Moscow.

KRASNICHAKOV

He had two strong convictions. One was that Siberia wasn't ready for Communism, and that even if it was it would be destroyed by the Japanese or by the Allies. Therefore, the only thing to do was to keep it a buffer state between Japan and the Soviets. To do this and placate all sides took infinite tact.

Tobinson proved equal to the task. His record in the last three years is a record of extraordinary achievement. He has established schools with the most modern methods; and against the most terrific odds he has slowly but surely made the life of the Far Eastern Republic one of steady, national reconstruction. I don't think he believed for a minute that it should be permanently separated from Russia.

LEO KAMINEV AND GREGORY ZINOVIEV

TOWARD the end of the first week of the Bolshevik uprising, Zinoviev and Kaminev lost heart. With Mylutin, Nogin and Rykov, they handed in resignations to the Central Executive Committee of the Communist Party. Lenin read the letters at a great meeting in Smolny and cried: "Shame upon these men of little faith, who hesitate and doubt!"

Lenin has long since conquered their opposition, but he has not changed their souls. Kaminev and Zinoviev are in his cabinet, as satellites, however, not as leaders; they are the weakest members.

Kaminev is President of the Moscow Soviet and a member of the All-Russian Central Executive Committee of Soviets. He is on the national famine committee and probably makes a very good impression on the American Relief people with whom he comes in contact. They ought to feel quite at home with him; he has the genial manners of an American small-town politician.

He has certainly retained a middle class consciousness in spite of five years of actual revolutionary experience, in spite of what is known in Russia as a steady revolutionary past. I don't think his idea of Communist discipline can be very well defined. He likes to be magnanimous and promises everything to everybody. He is generous, and since it is hard to be generous in a Socialist State where one owns nothing to be generous with, his only recourse is to be generous with the property of the State.

In a glow of hospitality he once gave a sable coat worth thousands of dollars to a lady he admired and was genuinely astonished and grieved, I think, by the bitter criticisms then hurled at him. Had there been enough "trusted and trained" men to go round (which there never are in any government), this particular attack of giving might have cost him his career, though in any other society his actions would have been quite normal.

Kaminev is an excellent subordinate and capable of making a fortune in a capitalist society. He cannot be accused of having no ideals; he can be accused only of having the average politician's moral stamina.

Bela Kun is the only other Soviet official who parallels Kaminev's distrust of the press. I once went to Bela Kun's office to get a statement. After ten promises and ten delays, I was in a small rage myself and asked him why he had not said in the first instance that he had no intention of giving a statement. He looked up from his desk, ran his chubby fingers through his hair, and said in a bewildered way, "Well, you see, I have just taken aspirin." A young Russian officer sitting nearby smiled at me and said dryly, in English, "No wonder the Hungarian Soviets fell!"

Kaminev will probably remain in office many years for no better or no worse reason than the reason for which many of our Senators are returned to Washington term after term.

Zinoviev's position is much more important and much harder to define. Aside from being in the Cabinet, he is President of the Petrograd Commune and President of the Third International. He really has great power and he is known to be wilful and arbitrary. His party opponents claim that his capriciousness has split the German Communist party into six factions and confused and alienated most of the parties in the other countries.

A Russian professor, who was interested in political movements merely as an observer, explained Zinoviev's curious tenacity in office in this way: "The Communists," he said, "insist so strongly upon party discipline and party loyalty that they have never been able to face the fact that Zinoviev is not a leader."

Zinoviev's appearance is against him. He is short, heavily built, flabby. Yet he is not devoid of vanity; he is the most photographed man in Russia. And while he has little imagination, he has real dramatic sense, he has a way of staging everything.

At Baku, at one moment he had the Easterners unsheathing their swords and declaring a holy war; at another moment he had a group of Mohammedan women in the gallery tearing off their veils. All this was distinctly impressive and dramatic, but the real drawback was that the effect of the second act almost ruined the effect of the first.

I often wonder if a man can be a great leader, and be utterly devoid of humor. When Zinoviev says anything clever he is not even aware of it and invariably spoils it by a second act.

During the Kronstadt uprising the Esthonian government, with its wish father to its thought, sent a wire to Petrograd which read: "What sort of government have you in Petrograd?" And

Zinoviev replied: "The same government that has been here since 1917."

If he could only have stopped at that one sentence he might have been able to lead a world revolution, or at least catch the imagination of the workers. Instead he insisted upon being didactic. He wired page after page, delivering an orthodox Marxian lecture! But the International is not without men of talent and daring. There are men under Zinoviev—Italians, Frenchmen, Germans, Bulgarians, Americans, with real fire and ability.

Bucharin, editor of *Pravda,* is by far the most brilliant of the Russians. No matter how much one may disagree with Bucharin, one must concede his brilliancy. The Letts have an exceptionally able group in the International. Some of these men were actually in power during the brief time that Latvia was "red." The leader of the group is a stately old man called Stootchka. For four months he was President of Latvia.

PETER STOOTCHKA

PETER STOOTCHKA is one of those advisers and assistants of Lenin that the world has not yet discovered. He is a man of capacious mind and one of Lenin's closest friends. He is a lawyer by profession and for many years was the editor of a Lettish progressive paper in Riga. He was exiled to Siberia for some criticism of the Tsar's government.

He was the first Commissioner of Justice under the Soviets and only resigned his post to accept one as President of Latvia. When Riga fell he went back to Moscow, took up quarters near Lenin in the Kremlin, and there he remains.

It was Stootchka who wrote the Soviet constitution, as well as most of the present laws. Evidently he did not always find writing laws an easy task. He often confessed his inability to judge just how the personal and family life would grow up around the great economic change which had taken place. Stootchka is nearly seventy and he felt that he might be a little old-fashioned in regard to some matters, especially concerning marriage and divorce. In the end he left it for those most concerned to decide.

One afternoon he called into his office five young Russian women, all typical revolutionists, and said to them: "For centuries women have been oppressed, they have been the victims of prejudice, superstition and the selfish desires of men. In writing the marriage laws I don't mind if women have even a slight advantage over men. What I am concerned with most is to see that they get full justice. So I have asked you here as representatives of the new order. Think these matters over and give me your conclusions."

Naturally, these conclusions had to be voted on by the All-Russian Congress of Soviets, but since they were passed and written, it is now an historical fact that five young women are the real authors of the new and rather free marriage laws.

ALIEXIEV IVANOVITCH RYKOV

No other Russian enjoys the solid political and popular backing of Aliexiev Rykov; he is the logical successor to Lenin.

Rykov is one of those "unknown-quantity" men which are in every government and every political party and who are on the "inside" of every government decision, men who silently assume more and more power but remain unknown to the press until some event brings them to the public attention. Rykov, although he has held for several years four of the most important posts in Russia, was never heard of in England or France or America until Lenin's illness brought to everyone's lips the question of who would be the next Premier. Rumor suggested Kaminev and Trotsky and numerous other Commissars. As Rykov himself explained to me, "none of these men could take Lenin's place for the very logical reason that they had held government posts which had nothing to do with the Premiership. It was like expecting one of your Secretaries of War or Navy to take your

President's place in case your President died or fell ill." Rykov, happening to be vice-Premier, automatically became acting-Premier. (Under the Soviets this office is called Chairman of the People's Council of Commissars.)

Rykov's background is interesting and worth knowing, since he will be a figure of importance in Russia for a long time to come. He is forty-one years old and, aside from being Premier, he is vice-Chairman of the Council of Labor and Defense, Member of the Presidium of the All Russian Congress of Soviets and Member of the Central Executive Committee of the Communist Party.

He was born of a peasant family living in the province of Vatka. His education was paid for by an elder sister who had married well. Because of revolutionary activities he was sentenced to Siberia and served seven years in *solitary confinement*. When he told me this, I was so astonished that I asked him to repeat it. It is a trial which would have broken almost any man; yet I think I never met a man with less "nerves" than Rykov has. By his manner and his good humor and his serenity, he resembles Lenin to a startling degree. It is rather amazing that Russia produced two men of the same type during the same period. That is one reason why the government machinery ran along so smoothly after Lenin stepped out.

Rykov has been in such close touch with Lenin in the last years that he almost anticipates Lenin's decisions. He told me that for three years he has been sharing Lenin's work. When the Council of Labor and Defense was formed during the blockade, Lenin headed it and Rykov and Alexander Demietrievitch Tsurupa served with Lenin. They also shared Lenin's work on the Council of People's Commissars; and when Rykov was temporarily elevated to Lenin's office, Tsurupa was elevated to Rykov's. As Lenin grew stronger, after his operation, Rykov went to the country about once a fortnight to consult him on vital matters of state. It is his opinion that Lenin will soon be back in the Kremlin. But if Rykov's prediction does not prove true, Rykov himself will be able to guide, with a steady hand, the shifting fortunes of war-torn and famine-ridden Russia. I do not think he will go down in history as a great figure; he will probably be overlooked by history as has many another such unselfish and solid builder of empire, who worked always in the shadow of a greater man.

JACOB PETERS, FEDORE S. DZERZHINSKY
AND THE
EXTRAORDINARY COMMISSION

JACOB PETERS, FEDORE S. DZERZHINSKY
AND THE
EXTRAORDINARY COMMISSION

IT IS a curious but indisputable fact that Jacob Peters, known to the world as "Peters, the Terrorist," has never been head of the Russian Extraordinary Commission. Since its inception, Fedore Dzerzhinsky has had charge of that sombre institution, which in the revolutionary vernacular is known as the "Cheka," a word derived from the initial letters of "extraordinary" and "commission."

Dzerzhinsky is a Pole, forty-four years of age, with an unusually classical background for a Chief Executioner. He ranks high even among the intelligentsia. After finishing his literary studies in a Russian university, he took post-graduate courses in Vienna, Berlin and Zurich.

He has a temperament much like Tchicherin; shy, aloof and deeply puritanical. One feels he can neither understand nor forgive moral weaknesses in others, since he himself possesses that

fanatical devotion which has made it possible for
him to travel the hard, bitter road where his ideals
lead. He asks nothing of life but to serve the
cause of Socialism. Ease, wealth and happiness,
he puts behind him as he would Satan. Such a
man can sign away life with an unruffled firmness
that would break one of a warmer temperament.
He needs only to be convinced that his course is
righteous; nothing else matters. The individual
is not considered in that "Nirvana" which is his
ultimate goal.

Dzerzhinsky adores Lenin and serves him with
the abject faithfulness of a slave; in his eyes Lenin
can do no wrong. In the first days of the terror,
he brought his doubts before Lenin, doubts which
had only to do with the effect of such measures
on the national and international political situation and not with his own soul. Lenin, when all
is said, is the only man who cannot afford to be
swayed by doubts. His responsibilities are those
of a field marshal during a battle; he has no
right to indecision. He reserves only the right to
change his tactics—which is quite another matter.

The terror was established in a moment when
the revolution was almost lost. The liberal government had fallen, the moderate Socialist govern-

ment had fallen. If the Bolsheviks fell, only chaos or a return to the monarchy was possible. So it was that when Dzerzhinsky came to the Kremlin and stood hesitating like a school-boy before his master, it was often Lenin who for the moment became the high lord of life and death.

I can see that scene in my mind's eye. In his hand Dzerzhinsky would have a list of prisoners and the evidence hastily gathered. Lenin would look at Dzerzhinsky's list, asking sharp, short questions in his shrewd way. Most of the names of the counter-revolutionary conspirators were familiar to him. He could quickly piece together the scanty evidence of the secret trials. In his mind thoughts like these must have traveled: "Ah, yes, there is X——— caught plotting with Y———, which, of course, entirely accounts for the rising at B———." Suddenly he would turn to Dzerzhinsky and say without excitement and without raising his voice: "It would be better to shoot these two, hold these five and release the rest."

In justice to Lenin it must be recorded that he was always against capital punishment for his political rivals, or even for those who plotted to assassinate him; he believed in the death penalty only for those who attempted forcibly to overthrow the government. His dictatorship of the Cheka, like his dictatorship of other government departments, ceased with the first semblance of order. At the same time, I do not believe for a moment that the Cheka ever got beyond his control. Recently, when he saw it growing into a power which interfered with the natural development of the country, he began at once to weaken it. Dzerzhinsky will no doubt assist him in such an undertaking with the same zeal which he brought to its creation. .

A good deal of political manœuvering has always been necessary in order to appease popular opinion about the Cheka. When time has cooled our emotions for and against the Communist idea, we will realize that Jacob Peters and Fedore Dzerzhinsky were just as much victims of the revolution as were those counter-revolutionaries who came under their stern jurisdiction.

Peters was sent away from Moscow in 1919 because he had become, however unjustly, a symbol of terror in the public mind and life was beginning to settle down again into more normal ways. As a matter of fact, Peters but countersigned orders already bearing the signature of Dzerzhinsky. It was his duty to see that the prisoners were quickly and humanely disposed of. He performed this grim task with a dispatch and an efficiency for which even the condemned must have been grateful, in that nothing is more horrible than an executioner whose hand trembles and whose heart wavers.

Pursuing the same devices, a few weeks back when Lenin forced the Cheka to be made subservient to the Department of Interior and Communications, the public looked upon this step as a real compromise and a definite move toward the abolition of the secret police. Trials again became public with employers and other unbelievers in Socialism openly represented by lawyers, who had long ceased to regard their profession as anything but a dead asset. Lenin never dismisses men he can trust, so while Dzerzhinsky ceased to be head of the once all-powerful Extraordinary Commission, he was elected in the same moment Commissar of the Interior and Communications, although temporarily he was sent to Siberia to expedite grain shipments for the famine areas. Thus the history of the Cheka repeats itself.

In the first moments of elation following the March revolution when prison doors were thrown open all over Russia and prison records publicly burned, it seemed as if the day of the secret police was forever passed. In those joyous days it was almost impossible to keep one's perspective, or to feel a premonition of the rising storm of world opposition to the development of the revolution. When Kerensky abolished the death penalty in the army, he sacrificed his last shred of control to the dictates of his heart. At that time even the Communists did not believe in capital punishment. Once Trotsky, in an impassioned speech at Smolny, during the November days, made mention of a guillotine. His remarks let loose the most violent opposition. For weeks this issue was discussed everywhere; in the press, at public gatherings, even in street cars and on railway trains. He was vigorously denounced for holding such opinions. And he had merely said that this was something to be considered in a national crisis.

By the summer of 1918 the Soviet government found itself surrounded by an iron ring of death. Also, there was graft and intrigue and dishonor in the Communist ranks. It was Peters himself, torn between the right and wrong of re-establishing capital punishment, who said to me in January, 1918, "If we ever have to kill, it must begin in our own ranks." His face was white and stern; he appeared on the verge of collapse.

"Will it ever really come to that?" I asked.

He passed his hand across his eyes with the weary gesture of a man who has not slept well for many nights. Before him on his desk, was a pile of papers. He pointed to them and said, "If you could know what evidence I have here, you would see how necessary it is if the revolution is to continue, for the Communists to purify their own ranks."

It is a matter of record that the first persons put to death were opportunists who pretended to believe in Communism and had accepted bribes or otherwise had betrayed their own party.

The momentum of the revolution rapidly increased after the signing of the first death warrant. It was not long before the despised secret police once more made their appearance. They were back again protecting now a revolutionary government as energetically as they once protected the Tsar!

It is impossible to say how many of the old police force actually served under the Soviets. I found, on personal investigation, that many of the stories were largely myths. The most typical

legend was the one concerning Lapochine, once
head of the Okrana and exiled by the Tsar for
telling a Social Revolutionist that Azef was a
spy. The rumor that he now holds an important
post in the Cheka is not true. His daughter was
one of my intimate friends in Moscow and I went
very often to her home. Her father was holding
two small clerkships which took all his time, in
order to get double rations to support himself and
his invalid wife. Lapochine was never connected
with the secret police after his exile, although he
was brought back to Russia after six years in
Siberia and publicly forgiven by the Tsar. He
was governor of Esthonia at the outbreak of the
revolution. However, to the ordinary individual,
all this makes little difference. A detective is
simply a detective, working in dark ways, someone to be feared and someone to be despised.
And as for the Lapochines, the last time I heard
of them they were trying to borrow money in
America to start a sausage factory near Moscow.

All the important posts in the Cheka have been
and still are largely held by Letts or Poles with
unimpeachable revolutionary records. The rank
and file are Russians. There are scarcely any
Jews. The reason why the Russians hold minor

positions is not exactly clear but the general calculation is that they are more susceptible to bribery and more easily influenced. Certainly, the Cheka has played an important rôle in the revolution; it is no exaggeration to state that without the vigilance of the Extraordinary Commission, the Soviets would never have maintained themselves through numerous critical moments. It was Peters and other Lettish secret agents who discovered such counter-revolutionary plots as the Lockwood plan to blow up bridges and cut off Petrograd and the government from all communications. And as military intervention developed, the Communists were forced to consider Russia in a state of siege and the Cheka their most necessary means of self-protection.

In a speech before a session of the Extraordinary Delegation, Trotsky made this statement: "The monopoly of using force and reprisals in any normally functioning state, regardless of its external form, is an attribute of the government. . . . Every state organization is in this way fighting for its existence. It is sufficient to picture to one's self the society of the present day, this complicated and contradictory co-operation in such a tremendous country as Russia, for example, in order at once to understand that in the present condition of affairs, torn by every social contradiction, reprisals are absolutely inevitable."

It is absurd to consider the Extraordinary Commission in any but an objective way. The little border states of Finland, Lithuania, Roumania, and even Poland, have just as elaborately developed Chekas, searching just as diligently for Bolshevik plotters as Russia does for anti-Bolshevik plotters. Finland, for example, has a much more cruel revolutionary record. The division of the Red and White forces there was more equal; therefore, the struggle was intensified and the terror magnified accordingly. Only, in this case, it was White Terror instead of Red.

Even we ourselves have a Cheka, but we call it a Department of Justice, and we have a thousand little independent Chekas known as private detective agencies. And now that America is in a happier state of mind we like to forget how our "intelligence" departments grew into formidable institutions during the short period of our participation in the war. Very soon after the declaration of war we began to suspect one another on a wholesale scale, all sorts of innocent persons were "trailed" and otherwise humiliated. If we remember those days, we can better understand what happens when the very life of a nation is at stake. Ours never has been.

No one claims that the state electrician who pushes the button for the electric chair at Sing Sing is a criminal, or that his private life need necessarily be immoral. Yet the Sing Sing executioner is paid something like three hundred dollars for each life taken and one might almost imagine him having more than a routine interest in a good crop of homicides. If Peters and Dzerzhinsky were dismissed from office to-morrow, they would have nothing but the clothes on their backs and broken health with which to begin new careers. I give this example for the sake of comparison or contemplation, not as a justification for either the American or the Russian official conscience.

The temptations of St. Anthony pale beside those of Peters and Dzerzhinsky. They have been flattered and offered every sort of bribe. I know of a single instance where Peters was offered what amounted to a cool million dollars. He did not refuse it, however, until he had all his tempters enmeshed beyond retreat.

The most romantic revolutionary story I know

is the one Peters told me himself about his return
to Russia, bound up as it was with Sir Roger Casement's execution. Up until the day of that unhappy event he was immersed in the life of London
and almost untouched by the struggle in Russia.
He had a comfortable post in an export house, an
English wife and a baby whom he adored. Quite
naturally thoughts of revolution had grown vague
and alien to his mind. So it was that, wrapped in
British complacency, on a gray morning he started
happily to work and encountered unexpectedly a
little company of Irish folk bound for the Tower
of London. At first he must have looked at them
as he would have regarded any other procession.
But he noticed, to his surprise, how emotional they
were. Tears ran down their faces of which they
were unashamed. He remembered then that this
was the day when Sir Roger Casement was to die.
Something, he said, made him follow that crowd,
although they were going in an opposite direction
from his office. Can you imagine the punctilious
Mr. Peters, so highly efficient, never a minute late,
for a reason unexplainable to himself, following a
little group of Irish mourners? Perhaps he had
even grown English enough to be a little embarrassed at his impulsiveness.

PETERS AND DZERZHINSKY

He described how he stood when the others knelt down outside the prison and began to pray. He would never forget, he said, how he suddenly realized what a vast, irreconcilable temperamental barrier lay between the English and the Irish people.

By the time the bugler announced the execution, Jacob Peters was another man. Something called conscience or national pride or revolutionary honor awoke in him and with it came a deep homesickness for Mother Russia. He felt himself burning with shame. It was as if Sir Roger Casement were pointing a finger at him and saying, "See how I am able to die, you who once called yourself a revolutionist." Those devout people reminded him of the Russian peasants; they had the potency of an old tune. We have all seen men weep over some dear, familiar melody.

Peters never went back to work. He walked the London streets all day, wandered along the docks, watched the great ships and thought about Russia. All the dreams of his youth returned. At night he went home and told his wife he was going to Petrograd.

It seems almost regrettable that Sir Roger Casement could not have known that in that multitude come to mourn his death, was a little London clerk who, by the power of association, was somehow transformed into one of the characters that now make Russian history.

Neither Peters nor Dzerzhinsky bear much resemblance to their revolutionary predecessor, Marat, the venomous public prosecutor of the French revolutionary days. Dzerzhinsky is far too reserved to be an orator and I doubt if he understands the meaning of revenge. He must have known all too well the horror of prison life ages before he became head of the prisons. He spent eleven years in a Warsaw prison, an experience which permanently wrecked his health.

Early in his confinement a spirit of religious fervor, manifested in self-sacrifice and humbleness, was evident. He wished to abase himself in the same way a priest does penance before God. He took upon himself the most repulsive tasks in the prison in order to save his fellow prisoners, such as washing floors and emptying refuse pails. His only reply when questioned was, "It is necessary that someone should perform the lowest tasks in order that the others may be relieved of them." And it was this man whose fate it was to perform the lowest and hardest tasks for the young republic.

PETERS AND DZERZHINSKY

The meek can be truly terrible in positions of authority, as can the virtuous, since ordinary souls feel no defense against them.

In appearance Dzerzhinsky is tall and noticeably delicate, with white slender hands, long straight nose, a pale countenance and the drooping eyelids of the over-bred and super-refined. I never knew anyone who was a close friend of Dzerzhinsky's; he has, perhaps, too secluded a nature to permit of warm and intimate companionship. He is as distinctly aristocratic as Peters is distinctly a man of the people.

Peters is short, snub-nosed and almost stocky in build, with bristling, short, brown hair. He has read a good deal but is by no means a littérateur. He is a workman risen above the mass, risen just high enough to be an excellent interpreter. He has played in these years since March, 1917, other important rôles than that of executioner. As Governor of Turkestan he has shown that he can create as well as destroy.

When Peters returned from England he went almost immediately to the front and joined a Lettish regiment. Because of his superior knowledge or his fervor he soon became a figure of importance among the soldiers. He was the favorite spokesman at the soldier meetings, which at that time were of great importance, since the soldiers were deciding very largely for themselves whether or not they would remain in the trenches. Even Kerensky found it necessary to take fortnightly trips to the front to argue and plead with them.

To certain men who once served in Peters' regiment, was some months later entrusted the keeping of the Royal Family. Every man in that guard was a Lett. As in other instances, had they been Russians, they might have shown more leniency or outright sentimentalism in a crisis. The Letts were instructed never to allow their royal prisoners to be rescued alive and the Letts are soldiers who understand the iron rules of military discipline.

Lenin has long put great trust in Peters. When he was in hiding during the first two months of 1917, Peters was in charge of that seclusion. Lenin's famous "Letters to the Comrades," which were sent out and printed broadcast, and caused so much havoc with the Provisional Government, were entrusted to Peters and his subordinates. Peters was very proud of this trust. Once he said to me when I was living on a little street just off Nevsky Prospect, "Lenin is not far from this house." Little did I comprehend what an important confidence that was!

Peters speaks English fluently. In 1917 he translated a life of Kerensky for me and over tea cups he told me many things about the revolution which I did not understand. I should never have believed, in those days, that this mild-mannered and almost inspired youth would soon have such sinister work to do.

The last time I met Peters he was living in Tashkent which is the capital of the Province of Turkestan. He had even more sweeping powers than an ordinary governor, since he was the most important revolutionary official in a community not yet settled down to normal life.

I also met the new Madame Peters. The English wife divorced him at the time of the terror. The second Madame Peters was a very pretty, red-headed Russian who had been a teacher and who still worked at her profession. They lived in a single room, shared a dining room with twenty others and were poorly dressed. When we discussed this point, Peters bitterly denounced several Soviet officials who, he said, were "living soft." "A revolutionist cannot expect to force privations on other people if he is not willing to be an example of self-sacrifice," he declared.

He had become known almost as a conservative among the Left-Communists because he had refused to close the Mohammedan bazaars, saying these people were not ready for Communism. His public trials were attended by large crowds and proved of great educational value in a very unenlightened community.

I found him much older. He seemed to have lived thirty years in three. He never mentioned the terror, nor did his wife, and I could not bring myself to. Only once did he indirectly refer to it. The three of us were starting to a local Soviet meeting. He picked up a revolver from his table and, for a moment, stood regarding it. Then he turned to me and said, "Have you ever used one of these?" I said, "Of course, I know how, but I've never had to." And then he exclaimed, "I wish to God I never had!" After all, what a story can be condensed into a single sentence!

The Cheka was really the beginning of law and order; it marked the beginning of the first government which showed real strength and purpose. There was no doubt something very definitely nationalistic about the growth of the Cheka, in spite of the fact that it was established by Communists. It had all the hardness of purpose and the narrowness possessed by the maximum of patriotism. Any student of history will remember what Carlyle said of those terror-ridden days when the guillotine ruled France. "Tigress nationale! Meddle not with a whisker of her! Swift rending is her stroke; look what a paw she spreads—pity has not entered her heart." Such acts Carlyle claimed would some day be known as the "Crimes of the Revolution," when they should rightly be recorded as the birth pains of the republic. Very naturally, conduct of open and avowed suppression will always be hated and condemned by liberals the world over, and used as campaign ammunition by political opponents.

One of the highest officials of the Cheka said to me, "Most foreign correspondents write about the Extraordinary Commission as if we had no right on our side. Now I will give you two examples of the sort of problems continually confronting us, and if you would submit them to any American police official, he would tell you very promptly that the Cheka had no other course than the one which it pursued.

"First, there is the case of Marie Spirodonova.

She is a woman with an honored revolutionary past. Naturally, we don't want to have her behind bars. But she was for years a terrorist, she killed the Governor of Tambov and she still believes that individual acts of terror are justified. As you know, the Communists were always against such a policy. We believe in mass action and not individual violence.

"Marie Spirodonova is a highly-strung, sensitive person. She makes a splendid agitator but we have gotten to the point of reconstruction, of building, not tearing down. Russia was forced to sign the Brest-Litovsk treaty. You may agree with me that that was a bad thing to do or you may disagree with me, but as an American, understanding and believing in government, you will certainly agree that we had to protect the representatives of Germany after the peace was signed.

"When Mirbach came to Moscow, it was very bitter for any of us to receive him. But it is another matter to go to his house and kill him with a bomb. This was the plan of Marie Spirodonova. Now what could we do? Were we to allow her and her associates to kill any foreign representative who came here? How could we ever hope for relations with other nations if we could offer their representatives no protection? Then why are we criticized because we put Spirodonova in a sanatorium? And we allowed her to escape. I confess that we have kept a watch over her. The woman in whose house she stayed used to report to us. That was merely to prevent any repetition of the Mirbach affair.

"One thing I wish the world could understand, one thing that my experience in the Cheka has taught me, that a person capable of starting a revolution is not necessarily capable of finishing one or even carrying one on after it is started."

Another time the same official gave me his version of the Anarchist problem. "We had Bill Shatov as Chief of Police in Petrograd. He was formerly an Anarchist but had come over to work with us. He had quarreled with the Anarchists and he claimed that a lot of loafers and thieves had joined their organizations just to have an excuse not to do any work.

"Some time later there were a lot of robberies in Petrograd. One night Bill Shatov arrested every so-called Anarchist in town. He held them two weeks without trial. In those two weeks not a single robbery took place in Petrograd!

"When the trial came up, Bill had a novel way

of trying cases. He put each man through a sort of Anarchist's catechism. All those who knew their litany he released—the others he held.

"Anarchists are the most difficult of all groups during a revolution. They not only lack balance and refuse to co-operate but they are really dangerous. There is hardly a Soviet official whose life has not been threatened by Anarchists. Twice, you know, they nearly finished Lenin.

"What does the outside world really expect us to do? We have to be especially vigilant now because these are harassing times. Later we will be no more formidable than your own police."

The Soviet Government has a passion for exhibits. The Labor Temple in Moscow almost all year round has about half its space devoted to educational displays. In a little room here I once saw a most curious and gruesome show. On the walls hung photographs of people executed for high treason, robbery and murder, with little cards attached giving the history of each case. In a corner were rifles of the type used in executing. There were also pictures of the victims of some of the criminals—pictures of Jews murdered in pogroms, for example, and of houses blown up. Any person from the street was allowed to go there quite freely, without any special pass, and acquaint himself with the workings of the committee.

There is always something appalling when one comes face to face with such a display of law and order. It reminds me of a very eccentric Russian doctor of my acquaintance. This man had a habit of killing flies. If he saw one on a window pane or hovering about the table he would somehow manage, with great deftness, to capture it. Thereupon he would solemnly take out his pocket knife and behead the insect. Once I protested, saying that such a performance was disgusting. With great seriousness he admonished me. "So, you do not believe in killing. . . . Well, nevertheless, we are all forced to kill. Flies annoy you, they poison your food, endanger your life and the lives of your children. In some desperate moment you strike out in a furious and chaotic manner. What is the result? Ugh, an ugly smash. Is there anything fine about that? You condemn me, but what do I do? I simply execute flies in a sanitary way—I am a true symbol of civilization."

ANATOL VASSILIEVITCH LUNACHARSKY AND RUSSIAN CULTURE

ANATOL VASSILIEVITCH LUNACHARSKY AND RUSSIAN CULTURE

"Oh, happy earth! Out of the blood of generations
  Life yet will blossom, innocent and wise,
And thou, my planet, shall be cleansed of lamentations,
  A jade-green star in the moon-silvered skies."

THUS wrote the Soviet Minister of Education, Anatol Lunacharsky, in those remote days when a revolution was only a vague goal and when he could not believe that in his own lifetime a day would come when he would be torn from his quiet study and forced to put his dreams into practice, or as near into practice as dreams ever reach.

Reality is revolting and disappointing to any artist, but Lunacharsky possesses enough recuperative powers to overcome his artistic sensitiveness. If he had not had enough also of that saving grace of fanaticism which marks all leaders, he would have lacked the enthusiasm which has carried him through every battle for culture which he has had to wage since the dramatic crash of the Tsardom. Only once did he actually lose heart

71

and Lenin overcame that attack of panic by showering responsibility upon him. Given responsibility he showed more courage than men of coarser grain.

Lunacharsky's battles in the five years he has been in office have not been concerned with bullets. "Illiteracy," he told me once, "is the great curse of Russia; we must fight illiteracy like the plague." And he fought it like the plague. This delicate poet, who in appearance is more like a scholarly Frenchman than a Russian, who has the manners and elegance of another age, has left off composing sonnets to fight ignorance, superstition, drunkenness, prejudice, disease, dirt. . . . And he has been more bitterly attacked than any other official of the new Russian Government.

With practically nothing at his disposal he had to plan and execute a vast educational campaign. That is why his achievements are so extraordinary. When Fedore Chaliapin was here last winter, winning the heart of America by his sweet and wonderful voice, he and I talked a good deal about Lunacharsky and the difficulties which confronted him. "Remember," said Chaliapin, "if you have no pens and no paper and no ink, you cannot write; if you have no wood you cannot make a fire—in

Russia all these things were literally true. Under such circumstances, no matter how willing the government might be, art and education must suffer with the rest."

I will not go into figures here, but one can get an idea of what Lunacharsky has done. He has practically eliminated adult illiteracy from the cities, he has established thousands of schools. Only a very few of them, to be sure, are up to the required mark, but every school opened is an achievement. And there is not a single part of Russia, however remote or however dark, where a school has not been started.

But establishing and maintaining schools and universities was only a part of the work allotted to Lunacharsky. He had to build new theatres, keep up the standard of the old and show himself worthy of that great responsibility Lenin bestowed upon him when he made him guardian of all the art treasures of Russia.

If Nikolai Lenin had been a mediocrity, he would never have appointed Lunacharsky guardian of the art of Russia, and Russian art would now be scattered to the four winds, swallowed up in private collections or enriching the pockets of speculators. A mediocrity will not admit his limitations even if he is aware of them, but Lenin somehow understands that a man cannot spend his life studying political economy and carrying on revolutionary propaganda, and at the same time be an art connoisseur. What is more remarkable is that he allowed Lunacharsky to tell him so. The story of Lunacharsky's appointment is interesting and characteristic of the Russian Premier's method of political generalship.

When the Red and White forces were struggling for the possession of the Kremlin in Moscow in 1917, a wire to Petrograd announced that the beautiful and fantastic church of Vassili Blazhanie on the Red Square had been razed to the ground. Lunacharsky, poet, scholar, playwright and revolutionist, as well as friend and follower of Lenin, wrote an open letter to the press in which he gave vent to his horror. He stated: "What is taking place in Moscow is a horrible and irreparable misfortune!" He wrote another letter to Lenin, renouncing all connection with the revolution. And he took to his bed, ill with shock and disappointment.

Lenin did not accept his resignation. Lenin never accepts resignations from men who are valuable to the state. Instead, he went to call on

Lunacharsky, and an amazing conversation took place which was repeated to me by a friend of both men.

Lenin, with his usual directness, said to Lunacharsky, "Do not be overcome by this calamity. If this church is destroyed, let us build a bigger and a better one."

Lunacharsky, in tears of anguish, explained to Lenin that such a thing was not possible; such a lovely, imaginative piece of architecture might never again be created. Lenin listened and went thoughtfully away. A few days later Lunacharsky was given charge of the entire art of Russia.

Up to that time, the valuable collections, as well as the buildings, had been in the hands of a revolutionary committee which also might very well have been of the opinion that art could be replaced by "bigger and better" things.

Lunacharsky did not take his task lightly. He issued another public declaration asking for the solemn co-operation of all loyal Russians. "Upon me rests the responsibility of protecting the entire artistic wealth of the people," he said, "and I cannot fulfill my duty without your help."

It will not be known for a long time against

what strong and subtle forces he had to battle to guard that trust. There was movement after movement to sell such treasures as the Rembrandt Collection in the Hermitage at Petrograd or the historic paintings and tapestries in Moscow. But Lunacharsky, ever on the alert, defeated every one of these attempts. He often fought bitter battles in his own party. Every possible sort of intrigue was manufactured against him. I remember times when he had to appear in public and defend himself against atrocious slander. Yet up to the present day he has saved absolutely everything except the pearls and diamonds of the royal family which, after all, were never of any particular artistic value. He saved even the Tsarist statues from the mobs that would have destroyed them, and stored them away in buildings for a calmer moment. He never lost his artistic perspective, art was always art and he "could look with a just regard upon the shattered corpse of a shattered king" provided that the monument was executed by a talented artist.

Nikolai Lenin has the genius to read men well; he recognized instantly that a man who could be so affected by the rumored loss of a single historic building that he could scarcely bear to face life, would be the very man to defend passionately the art of the nation. And Lenin has continued to defend Lunacharsky against every charge brought by his enemies. These charges have often been serious because they were brought by revolutionists who claimed that Lunacharsky was partial to the bourgeoisie in his efforts to get extra rates for scientists and artists; that he was not a real Communist because he put art before political propaganda. There was a terrible period when the loyalty of all men was questioned whose allegiance was not wholly given to the defense from military attack at whatever cost to art or personal life. It was through that period that Lunacharsky had to guide Russian culture.

"Think what vitality the theatre had to possess," said Chaliapin, "to maintain itself through the revolution." "Think what hunger the Russian masses had for learning," said Madame Lenin, "that they could grasp even this hard moment to learn to read and study." Both these assertions are true, but in spite of that hunger and that vitality both forces might have gone down for some years, had it not been for the splendid leadership of Lunacharsky.

Even those ardent revolutionists who could

see no further than the immediate moment are beginning to realize that the very fact that the
Soviets have kept intact their national art gives
them a prestige which money could never buy; it
is an indisputable evidence of their faith in civilization. And it is Lunacharsky who has managed
to save for them this evidence of faith when hot-
heads would have cast it aside.

It always seems a pity that we are aware now
of only the prominent political figures in Russia.
If we can think back on the French guillotine days
and the burning of libraries, the mad destruction
of art, the sacking of palaces by angry mobs, we
can understand that if there had been men in
France in those days who could have held those
mobs in check and made them want to read the
books they were burning, made them turn the
palaces into museums, Napoleon might never have
worn a crown. In Russia the influence of the men
who hold the political reins would be so much
slighter and so much less significant if they were
not backed up by men like Lunacharsky.

He had the art galleries heated in the most bitter of the fuel famine days and the immense
crowds going in partly to keep warm strolled all
day under historical canvases and came to know

all the great pictures of Russia. The Winter
Palace became a Revolutionary Museum, one of
the most unique museums in the whole world, the
Palace of Nicholas II at Tsarskoe Selo became a
Children's Home, as did every great estate in the
provinces threatened with destruction by quarrel-
ing peasants.

It is interesting to note that the wives of three
prominent revolutionists rendered Lunacharsky
valuable aid in his difficult work, the wife of
Trotsky, the wife of Gorky, and the wife of Leo
Kaminev.

Madame Trotsky has under her direction all
private art collections and all the small palaces;
she hands a monthly inventory of these places over
to Lunacharsky. In the last three years she has
been very gradually and systematically removing
the most valuable objects in the collections to the
museums.

Madame Kaminev, Trotsky's sister, is the head
of Prolocult, a movement which aims at a new
culture, especially in the theatre, which is free
from Greek or other influences. It is Madame
Kaminev's theory that such a culture, springing
from the workers and peasants and unspoiled by
the imperfections and influences of former civ-

ilizations, will do much to stimulate and renew art in general, which she believes has become decadent.

Marie Andreeva (Madame Gorky), who is herself an actress of note and was at one time a star in the famous Art Theatre in Moscow, had charge of Narodny Dom, a people's theatre, which was started under the Tsar and is continued under the Soviets. Marie Andreeva recently made a tour of Europe to study the theatres.

But it is Stanislavsky, the director of the Moscow Art Theatre, who has rendered Lunacharsky the greatest assistance. Stanislavsky is conceded to be the greatest stage director in the world. Under his guidance, all the great Russian playwrights for the last generation have blossomed. It was Stanislavsky's firm conviction that the Russian people must maintain the theatres, hundreds of theatres, during the revolution, in order that they might not find a life of hunger and cold too monotonous for a desire to live. With his brave little company he has managed to keep his theatre in the capital at the very highest pitch. He established and kept under his direction three other theatres in Moscow and he has put on a number of new operas. Absolutely nothing seems to discourage him. The loss of his personal fortune, which had been very great, and even the loss of his beloved workshop which was turned into a Chauffeurs' Club, did not destroy his calm. "It is never Lenin or Lunacharsky, big men, who are to blame for these mistakes of the Soviet Government," he told me. "It is always the little foolish, frantic men. When they took my workshop I wrote to Lenin. He did everything he could and when he was out-voted by Kaminev and the Moscow Soviet, he managed to get me another place, really just as good but lacking the old atmosphere."

Many tales could be told about Lunacharsky. The most typical, I think, and the one that shows his persistency is the story of the Hermitage museum, which Catherine the Great founded in Petrograd.

When the Germans were knocking at the gates of Petrograd in 1917 the historic tapestries in the Winter Palace and the entire Hermitage collection were sent by dead of night to Moscow and stored in the Kremlin. One day in the winter of 1921 I called at Lunarcharsky's office. He was in a fine state of happiness. "I have great news for you," he exclaimed. "To-day we sent the Her-

mitage collection back to Petrograd—intact! I
wonder if you can realize what that means? I
wonder if the world will know how nearly those
precious things came to destruction? How wonderful it is, after all, that in another month one
can go to Petrograd and behold everything arranged as it has been for centuries.

"Yes, there have been times when I did not
think it possible to save the collection, not because
there were reckless revolutionists who always
brought up movements to sell one part or another,
but by a much worse destruction. Can you imagine
my anxiety when fighting, actual fighting, was going on in palaces where the old porcelains were
stored? We had put the Rembrandts and other
canvasses in the Kremlin cellars, and I was in con-
stant terror that rats would gnaw them. Sometimes I was afraid to go down and look. But I
feel that the worst days of such struggles are over
for us. I am happy that Russia has demonstrated
to the world that Russians are not barbarians. We
have saved our art in spite of hunger and disease
and death."

Lunacharsky has a rare grace of spirit and
while he is himself a modernist and wants to bring

art as close to the people as bread, he never allows his own feelings to intrude on the feelings of his fellow artists. Himself a writer of note, he has sacrificed his own writing to save art and the creators of art. A devout revolutionist, he can allow the intricate designs of the Tsardom, the great black eagles, insolent against the sky over the turrets of the Kremlin, to remain, because they are part of the original designs of the old palaces. He can bring himself to regild the church roofs from his scanty funds although he is not at all religious, and he could faithfully gather old ikons and make of them a marvelous little collection in one of the new museums. Only such a man could have held together the temperamental army composed of the artists of Russia. Such men as Lunacharsky give the revolution the balance which prevents its collapse.

Periods of transition are always bitter and more than bitter for delicate creative souls. Once I mentioned Lunacharsky's tact in handling artists to Helena Soochachova, the young and beautiful star at the Moscow Art Theatre. She smiled and thus characterized him: "Ah, Lunacharsky," she said, "he is a great gentleman, he is, no doubt, *the* great gentleman of the revolution. That is the secret of his success and the reason his political enemies cannot defeat him and we artists cannot desert him—because he struggles so magnificently and is a man *sans peur et sans reproche.*"

MICHAEL IVANOVITCH KALININ

AND THE

PEASANTS

KALININ

MICHAEL IVANOVITCH KALININ
AND THE
PEASANTS

THERE have been two presidents of the Russian Socialist Federated Soviet Republic; only recently we have become vaguely aware of one of them. Ever since the Bolshevik *coup d' état* America has spoken of the Soviet Government as "the government of Lenin and Trotsky." America was right in so far as these men enjoy immense power, and wrong in so far as she imagined it would have been possible at any time, and less so now, for either of these men or both of them to have abruptly changed the government's policy from right to left or left to right without first receiving indisputable orders from the masses.

Relatively, Lenin has more power than Lloyd George and Trotsky considerably less; while President Kalinin, who began his office as little more than a figure-head, has been saved from the emptiness of such a position because he is so symbolic of the growing power of the peasants. Al-

ready more power has been bestowed upon him
through the course of events than perhaps he himself realizes. Surely when he set out in his painted
train on his first journey through the provinces
three years ago, he could hardly have foreseen his
place in history as one of the greatest influences
in molding the new state.

Kalinin's growing influence is a true barometer
of public opinion or, to be more exact, of the re-
assertion of public opinion. And it is interesting
to note that while many of the stars in the Communist sky are considerably dimmed by the as-
cendancy of Kalinin, Premier Lenin's position is
only made stronger. This is because the new
pressure from below is for compromise, and public
men go down under retreat much faster than when
their banners are flying triumphantly in advance.
Lenin is practical enough to understand the ad-
vantages of a well-ordered retreat above those of
a rout; he will save all he can of the Socialist
state instead of abandoning it on the fields of
battle.

It was the question of private property which
became the vital issue in 1920 inside and outside
of Russia. The abolition of private property was
made possible by a determined, conscious minor-

ity. It was re-established by the pressure of a slow-moving, solid, unconscious majority; that majority was the peasants. I do not mean that the peasants are now actually in control of the state. I merely wish to point out that they already hold the balance of power and that they move towards control with the crushing surety of a glacier. They hold, strategically, the same position that the Bolsheviks did under Kerensky, but they will never pursue the same tactics; they will assume power gradually just because they are the majority; it is only a minority which must act with dramatic haste, counting on brains, daring and psychological moments.

It was logical that the first President should have been a man who represented the city workers and the second President, a peasant; for in such wise did the revolution settle itself.

Most of the Communists did not approve of Kalinin's election. Lenin alone sensed the proper time to place a peasant as nominal head of the Soviets; a peasant who should begin as Master of Ceremonies and who, in his peasant's garb and with his peasant's tongue, should bring Lenin's ideas to the people; a peasant who would never cease being a peasant and who would come back to Lenin and say, "This and this they will have, here they cannot follow and there they will lead." Lenin gazed at Russia through Kalinin's eyes as one gazes in a crystal.

In 1917 when the Bolsheviks seized control of the state, a delicate little man called Jacob Michaelovitch Sverdlov, a chemist by profession and a revolutionist by conviction, was Chairman of the Central Executive Committee of the Workers and Soldiers Deputies; this meant that he controlled the Red Guards, the conscious workers and the revolting soldiers; it meant he held a position of such tremendous authority that he could not be ignored by anybody. So when the first Council of the People's Commissars was formed, which is really no other than the cabinet of the Russian Government, Sverdlov was the first person taken into consideration by them. And in order to find a place for him they created the office of President. When he accepted that office he gave up his direct control and became but one voice in a group. Nevertheless, all through the barricade days he continued to act as the spokesman in the cabinet for the Petrograd workers who were, for at least the first year, a power above the cabinet.

KALININ

In the winter of 1918 Sverdlov died of typhus and was buried on the Red Square in Moscow.

During the time Sverdlov was president the government was in continual difficulty with the peasants. They resisted the government's requisitioning expeditions, retreated within themselves and almost ignored the central power until the provinces were in a continual state of guerilla warfare. They managed their local Soviets with little or no thought of the Moscow Government. Civil war continued and, with the aid of France and England, grew apace; hard dark days settled over Russia. Sverdlov looked about for an entering wedge which would somehow pierce the way to an eventual understanding and co-operation with the local and central Soviets. In this search Sverdlov discovered Kalinin. Kalinin was already immensely popular with the peasants; he had been on every Land Committee of importance since the beginning of the first revolution, under both Miliukov and Kerensky. During his term of office Sverdlov used Kalinin as a mediator in many difficult situations and Lenin watched his work with interest. An old Communist explained Kalinin's election in these words: "He was a 'find' of Sverdlov's, but it was Lenin alone who realized that days might come when he would be invaluable in holding Russia together." Those days have come; they came with the tightening of the blockade and continued with the famine.

Kalinin is a Communist, a brand of Communist differing as much from Zinoviev or Litvinov as Borah differs from Hughes or Hughes differs from Root; yet Hughes and Borah and Root are Republicans steeped to the bone in party discipline, rampaging now and then, but never dreaming of breaking away from the party. Kalinin believes in a kind of Communism, modified enough to suit the peasants, and Zinoviev believes in a kind of Communism that is suited, at any time, only for the advanced and conscious city proletariat.

Kalinin was born in the little village of Volost and still calls it his home, still has his little strip of land there. He was brought up religiously, and understands what the Church means to a devout Russian and never throws aspersions on it. Though not religious himself, he tolerates religion with the grave tolerance which never offends.

His old mother is outspokenly anti-Bolshevik, yet very much likes to have her say in the Volost Soviet. She is angry with the Bolsheviks because they are not religious. She scolds her son and pretends that she is not at all flattered because he is President of Russia and obviously believes that no honor is too great for him. She is always glad to talk to visitors about him and goes on monotonously repeating the same ideas in the manner of the aged: "No, I am not surprised," she will say, "that Michael Ivanovitch has gone so far. He was always studious, sitting up reading by candle-light after everyone else was in bed. And he was always saying to me, 'Don't bother me, mother, I've got lots of work to do.' That's the way he talks to me now when I lecture him about religion. But he's a good son and kind to everybody . . . only he certainly ought to think more about God."

I don't believe that Kalinin is ambitious; I think he would like nothing so much as to go back to his farm and live there the simple life of the village. When Lenin convinced him that it was his duty to be the voice of the peasants, he accepted the post in the quiet way of a man who has no thought of personal glory. There is nothing in his record that would prove him to be anything but entirely unselfish, and I have seen him when he was like one inspired. During the Kronstadt revolt he walked into that hostile city as he might walk into the mouth of a cannon. Yet no one dared or desired to harm him!

Kalinin is an old revolutionist. In his early youth he found himself unable to tolerate, without protest, the tyranny of the Tsar's government which manifested itself in such brutal cruelty towards the peasants. He has always been desperately poor, a real proletarian peasant, hoping to be rid one day of his endless debts and support himself and his family honorably and decently. He was forced through poverty to go to the city, where he worked in factories in winter; only the summers he spent with his family. These winters in the city, where he was thrown in contact with city workers, gave him an understanding of the psychology and desires of the city workers as well as of the peasants.

He was exiled to Siberia but not to hard labor, and he spent this enforced and only leisure of his life rounding out his education; mixing the classics with his dreams of freedom for Russia.

Kalinin's wife is an educated, energetic peasant, who has by her own ability become a figure of importance in her village; capable and strong and intelligent, she has managed her tiny farm just a little better than her neighbors and has been elected President of the Volost Soviet. It is a position of which she is immensely proud.

Madame Kalinin is an individualist; a modern feminist of the type of professional woman who, in America, insists on keeping her name and continuing her work after marriage. During the last three years she has been so busy that she has had no time to visit Moscow. Kalinin, on his rare vacations, has had to go to her. If she ever does visit Moscow she will surely wear her kerchief and her sheepskin coat. No doubt supercilious Russians are already saying that "Main Street has arrived in Moscow," just as we have been saying since March, 1921, that "just folks" are in the White House.

And there is a curious similarity between President Harding and President Kalinin; both were elected to represent the average citizen. In Russia average citizens are peasants—a ninety per cent average. Both presidents go about their home towns slapping fellow citizens on the back. Both were elected as figureheads for a party and both have already proven themselves a little more forceful and important than the party reckoned.

If Russia continues in the path where it is now, in fifty years the Kalinins will have become

Hardings, at home in silk hats and frock coats, as well as in sheepskins and high boots. But it is hard to predict where Russia is going or where the world is going.

When Kalinin rides through the provinces on his propaganda train carrying stocks of literature, a motion picture apparatus and his official seal, with the outside "done" by some futurist artist in garish colors and depicting a millennium in which Kalinin would not be at home, he is "Comrade" Kalinin to the whole train; he takes his meals with the train crew, the porters and the secretaries; all share alike. But the remarkable thing is that when he gets back to Moscow he makes no effort to shake the dust of the provinces from his boots, he rather makes a point of remaining distinctly a villager. He receives you in his Moscow office wearing the same old mended spectacles, the same threadbare coat and, I am sure, the same heart and mind. He brings the country along with him, invades the city with it, permeates it, overcomes it. . . .

This attitude is characteristic not only of Kalinin, it is characteristic of any peasant. I have often noted the delegates at the Congresses. They are neither shy nor bewildered, they sit solemnly in their places in the great hall, pondering all that Lenin says of trade or reconstruction, approving or disapproving; getting closer every day to the idea that Russia is theirs.

It is generally believed that the line between the city workers and the peasants is wide and irreconcilable, whereas there is actually no line at all. The city workers are only peasants who have gone to the city just as Kalinin did, when they could not make a living in the villages. Russian peasants never get over being farmers. Last winter I came upon an excellent example: Some three hundred skilled Russian mechanics from Detroit arrived in Moscow; they were sorely needed in the Russian factories. Without a single exception they refused to remain in the city! And when they learned that they might be conscripted and forced to stay they fled hurriedly in every direction. With one voice they exclaimed, "We came home to the land!"

Naturally, the government was in despair; officials were at a loss as to what measures could be taken to bring pressure and a sense of duty upon the returning Russians. Orators were sent to argue with the next group, but without success. The only solution the government found workable was to organize them before they arrived; to see that they brought tools from America and came with the definite idea of remaining in the cities for a fixed period; for only the country is real to the peasant, the city is forever an artificial, unhealthy invention.

Kalinin's office in Moscow is not in the Kremlin. To get into the Kremlin requires too much red tape. Therefore, while the President eats in the Kremlin dining-room which is just an ordinary Soviet mess-room, and sits in the Councils of the People's Commissars, he receives his army of callers in an ordinary office building in the heart of the city. One needs no pass or credentials to get in; one needs simply to walk up a flight of stairs, open a door and emerge into a large bare reception room full of noisy peasants; here he inevitably turns up.

I have often thought that Kalinin's office is the most curious place in which I have ever been in my life; it has the atmosphere of a Russian railway train deep in the heart of the provinces where every passenger talks to every other passenger and where formality is not just overlooked or forgotten but has simply never existed.

All day long he receives the never-ending string

of peasants in the manner of a village priest, giving consolation and advice—and something more solid and satisfying than a prayer, for he is obligated to make an immediate decision in each case on hand or a promise that it shall be taken up through his office. Under no circumstances can he appear indifferent or helpless.

I remember arriving early one morning to find about twenty peasants ahead of me. When Kalinin came in everyone got up and there was a sudden general stampede in his direction and a sort of clamor which arises in any Russian household over any sort of argument. Kalinin's voice could be distinctly heard above the others shouting, "Comrades, comrades, I must take you in turn." Then, as he crossed the floor towards his private office, a frail, middle-aged woman sitting near the door burst into tears. I can see him now with his narrow Slav eyes, his broad nose and rumpled hair, his work-knotted hands and faded blouse, stopping to look through his spectacles at the woman before him, kindly, sympathetic, puzzled. . . .

I think that he knew even before he began to question her that hers was one of those unavoidable, personal tragedies that are part of change

and war and revolution. She had owned a big
country house, but the peasants had taken it when
they divided the land and they had allotted her but
two rooms to live in. She was humiliated, discouraged and resentful. She cried out, forgetting
that Kalinin was also a peasant, "I can't bear to
see those creatures using my pretty things, walking
with great muddy boots in my house. My soul is
in that house!"

Kalinin shook his head. He seemed willing and
even anxious to help her but he seemed more like
a doctor in that moment than an executive. Very
gently he asked her to remember that two rooms
were more than most people had now in Russia,
that these were difficult times; even so they would
go over the case together if she would wait her
turn. But no sooner had he closed the door than
every peasant in the room began addressing the
bewildered woman. They said that she should be
ashamed of such petty complaints and accused her
of asking for "special privileges." The widest
range of arguments were put forward, from the
man who had lost a cow and considered the government responsible to the woman whose two sons
had been killed at the front.

I was not so much interested in the arguments

as in the remarkably true reflection which the scene presented of what had happened all over Russia. I had never realized before how completely submerged the upper classes had become; how ruthless and inevitable was the vast upward surge of the peasantry. Here was this woman, one time *barishna* (lady), crushed and defeated in her own village, finding the same thought in Moscow as in Nizhni-Novgorod or Kazan or Baku.

When Kalinin called her she went forward but one could see that she had already given up hope and would not fight any further; perhaps for the first time the real significance of the revolution had become clear to her.

It is hard for Americans, where a peasant population has never existed, to realize the position of the peasants in a revolution. They are the rock in the whirlpool. They are the great levellers, the great destroyers as well as the great builders. In Russia they pulled down everything about them and they were not always gentle in their wrath. Often they ruined wilfully and needlessly. In the cities, practically no buildings were destroyed and no treasures looted, but in the provinces men often remembered the knout with red flames of fire and even with death.

Because the peasants' desires are simple, the world is apt to give them credit for a deep, political wisdom which they do not possess and while there is no doubt about their taking the business of government seriously, their inexperience often leads them into grave blunders. It was the peasants, and not the Communists, who most stubbornly opposed recognition of the foreign debts. It was the peasants who demanded from every government since the Tsar's, schools, hospitals and protection from invasion, but who always resented the most ordinary and reasonable tax put upon them by the central authorities. Until Kalinin had educated them they were wont to ask like children, "Aren't we free now? Can't we be left alone?"

The great irony about the rising of the peasants is that they were the first to abandon the very equality they fought for. The equalization of property in the provinces was brought about through the workings of peasant proletariat organizations known as Committees of the Poor, which not only divided the estates of the rich landlords but broke the power of the *kulaks* (rich peasants). When the whole country was reduced to the same status, the peasants were faced with the necessity of a great decision. There were no longer rich peasants or proletarian peasants but only what is known in Russia as the "middle" farmers. The question of how to maintain such an equality now arose. The Communists urged them to abandon the idea of private property and work the land in communes, pointing out that any other course must inevitably lead to the re-establishment of all the old values and a new bourgeoisie. But the peasants were afraid of this new and untried road of Socialism. Their demands for trade, silver money, the opening of markets and stores, are ample evidence that they have turned back on to the old familiar road of capitalism. If Russia had been an industrial instead of an agricultural country, the decision of the masses might have been quite otherwise.

Even our own presidents know the value of a lecture tour in a national crisis. In our immediate political past, we have the memory of presidents who took "issues" to the people, but it is hard to conceive of a Chief Executive lecturing almost steadily for over two years. Yet that is even a short estimate of the time actually spent by Kalinin in going from one end of Russia to the other, shuttling in and out of Moscow.

His meetings were more like tribunals, people's

courts, than ordinary political assemblies. The peasants gathered at the railway stations, in the village squares or even in the fields. They heard what he had to say and then he heard them. They argued, complained, demanded, compromised. Always some sort of understanding was arrived at. This was partly due to Kalinin's wonderful tact, his almost divine reasonableness which never allowed an argument to develop into a quarrel. And partly because he knows the peasant mind which is easily touched by stories of suffering, by flattery or tears, but impossible to move by threats. But fundamentally, the secret of Kalinin's success is due to the fact that he himself is a peasant and no walls of caste can exist between him and the people.

I can illustrate this feeling of complete contact best by the story of an actual occurrence in a remote province. It happened in what are now known as the worst of the "requisitioning days" when the Soviets were holding hundreds of miles of battle front and the peasants were taxed almost beyond endurance.

One day a Lettish officer, who was also a Commissar in some Red Army division, arrived in a remote village and rang the church bell to summon the people. He read a list of the goods to be requisitioned. This village had been taxed only a short time before and there were murmurs of dissatisfaction in the crowd, murmurs which grew into roars. Then happened one of those savage, elemental tragedies which even we in America have never been able to eliminate from our national life. Threats against the Commissar were followed by sudden violence; he was literally trampled to death.

The Lettish officer had been accompanied by a young peasant soldier, who had been a sort of orderly to him for nearly a year. In the struggle the boy escaped. All night he lay weeping and thinking of his dead comrade. The officer had taken an interest in him, had taught him to read and write and imbued him with the ideals of the Red Army. The peasant boy had been an orphan, lonely and unhappy and a victim of brutality. He thought now of the dead man as he thought of a saint, and by the time morning came he had resolved on a curiously brave act. Creeping into the church he rang the bell; the crowd gathered, and he mounted the platform and began to tell them of the dead man and the Red Army. It was not hard for him to explain that unless the Red Army was supported, the White forces would very soon take away by main force the very food they now refused to their brothers. It did not take very long to convince the crowd of peasants, and not only to convince them but to reduce them to tears. They gave all that the peasant boy asked, and more than that, they went solemnly in a procession to the fresh grave of the man they had murdered, laid wreaths upon it, and paid homage, saying: "Brother, forgive us, we could not see your heart."

This feeling accounts for the lack of resentment towards Kalinin when he goes into the famine area. He walks among the starving peasants, saying, "Who lies down, dies. I know, I have hungered, I am one of you."

In prosperous districts he uses the same tactics in overcoming opposition to collections for the famine. Whenever he finds local Soviet officials unwilling to part with their last surplus grain, he mournfully exclaims, "Ah, well, I am sorry to hear this! Last week I saw with my own eyes thousands dying of hunger. They were peasants like ourselves and they were calling to us to help. Will you send me back now with empty hands?" The peasants can never resist his appeal; it comes too close to them, it is like refusing one's father.

KALININ

While the peasants were not able to bring themselves to renounce their title to the land, they have otherwise quite whole-heartedly accepted many broad formulas of the Socialists. They unanimously approved of revolutionary Russia's offer to the world in 1917 to build a peace on the basis of "no annexations, no indemnities and the right of self-determination." It is a curious and sad reality that the richer nations become and the more cultured, the less they find it possible to comprehend such a simple recipe for justice and brotherly love. The world was too educated or too selfish or too frightened to accept Russia's magnanimous offer. And how much agony and bloodshed it might have saved!

The Russian peasants, who for so many centuries have struggled and sacrificed themselves to possess the land, are strangely lacking in national pride, as we know it. They are not envious of other countries. They could not conceive of an aggressive policy. If you say to them that America is far richer and more progressive than Russia, they will tell you they are very glad to hear it and are glad you are happy. They ask of the foreigner only to be let alone and not to send any more White generals against them; they ask to be allowed to develop their own political institutions. Obviously our only duty is to help them through their terrible struggle against the great famine which has come upon them like a curse through no sins of their own.

It is no miracle that President Kalinin can go freely about Russia, for no one is thinking of assassinating him. What would it profit enemies of Soviet Russia to kill a peasant like Kalinin? Are there not a million Kalinins? To sweep the Kalinins out of Russian political life would be like sweeping back the sea. To destroy the Soviets would be to destroy Russia. Even Sir Paul Dukes, of the British Secret Service, agrees that Soviets are the natural offspring of the revolution, conceived years ago under the Tsardom. Michael Ivanovitch Kalinin reflects the new Russia more faithfully than any other Government official.

MADAME ALEXANDRA KOLLONTAI

AND THE

WOMAN'S MOVEMENT

KOLLONTAI

MADAME ALEXANDRA KOLLONTAI
AND THE
WOMAN'S MOVEMENT

MADAME ALEXANDRA KOLLONTAI believes that everything which exalts is good; being a feminist, she exalts women. She tells women that they are capable of a new freedom, beautiful and unexampled. She is so carried away by her enthusiasm that she is unmindful of how easily wings are broken in this age of steel. But if her inspiration, which aims to lift women to the skies, lifts them only from their knees to their feet, there will be nothing to regret. Civilization, in its snail-like progress, is only stirred to move its occasional inch by the burning desire of those who will to move it a mile. And when faith is pure enough it does not demand realization.

Kollontai is like a sculptor working on some heroic figure of woman and always wondering a little why the slim, inspired, unmaternal figure of her dreams is forever melting back into a heavy, earthy figure of Eve.

It often happens that a character is best portrayed by conversations which show the manner of mind. In this chapter I have quoted Madame Kollontai at some length because she is the only articulate voice of the new order for women which has been so greatly misunderstood outside of Russia; that order which claims that by consecrating oneself to the state one lives truer to oneself and to others.

As champion of her sex, she cries to the women of Russia: "Cast off your chains! Do not be slaves to religion, to marriage, to children. Break these old ties, the state is your home, the world is your country!"

And who are the women she thus extolls? They are the women of the factories and the fields; the women who sweep the streets, who scrub, who carry heavy burdens, who plow and weave and drudge. Will they be able to follow her to such heights? By our logic, no, but Kollontai preaches a new logic for Russia.

Besides, we must consider just what she means by "casting off chains." I have heard her say all this another way and it did not sound so lofty or impossible. To an individualist, it did not even sound attractive. Last summer she admonished a women's congress in this manner: "We must build a new society in which women are not expected to drudge all day in kitchens. We must have, in Russia, community restaurants, central kitchens, central laundries—institutions which leave the working woman free to devote her evenings to instructive reading or recreation. Only by breaking the domestic yoke will we give women a chance to live a richer, happier and more complete life."

The material which Kollontai is so passionately attempting to mould is the peasant mind. It seems to me that peasant women are naturally slow-moving and stolidly honest and will accept only as much of Kollontai's philosophy as they find compatible with or necessary to the immediate situation; not because they are lacking in spirituality, for they are capable of deep religious fervor, but simply because much of it would be inharmonious and artificial to their normal development. At present her mission is to awaken them so that they may build a truth of their own which need by no means be a lesser truth than Kollontai's. If she attempts to make them swallow her formula intact she will certainly fail. If she compromises as Lenin compromises and as Kalinin does, she will perform for Russia a never-to-be-forgotten task.

To-day everything has been melted down in the crucible of the revolution. The only banner-bearer who counts is the one who will give to the great mass of those emerging into the new day the broad fundamental things of life.

Madame Kollontai is the only woman who has ever been a member of the Russian Cabinet. She puts forth the argument that women have more conscience than men and therefore do not attempt to obtain offices which they are not fitted for by previous training, and that this is the reason woman's influence is so slight in Russia to-day. But her history refutes her theory. She herself was particularly fitted for the position of Minister of Welfare. Her record was splendid. She lost her post because she was a woman and allowed her love for her husband to interfere with her political judgment.

Early in 1918, Madame Kollontai, who was the widow of a Tsarist officer, married Fedore Dubenko, the picturesque leader of the turbulent Kronstadt sailors. Dubenko is a handsome, daring young man, some years her junior. Shortly after the wedding Dubenko was arrested. He had entrusted certain ships under his command to officers of the old régime who had pretended loyalty to the Soviets, but who had turned the ships over to the Germans without a struggle. Certainly Dubenko had no intention of betraying the revolution, he was merely trying to make use of skilled officers, of whom there was a pressing dearth. Nevertheless, he was held responsible.

While he was in prison awaiting trial, Kollontai made rather violent and conspicuous protests both publicly and privately. As a result she was removed from office. Revolutionists have no tolerance for romance among their leaders during critical moments; they place the revolution far above personal relationship. From the beginning they looked with disapproving eyes upon Kollontai's infatuation for Dubenko.

When Dubenko was released, Kollontai went abroad and spent some months in Sweden. On her return she threw herself into a new work—that of educating her own sex to take an active part in politics.

Rightly speaking, there never was a woman's movement in Russia until after the revolution. Equal suffrage came first and political education afterwards. This condition appears particularly curious when one recalls that, during some years before the revolution, even more women than men were sent to Siberia for plots against the Tsar's government. Yet when the revolution came women sank mysteriously into the background. Russians explain this by various theories. One was that Russian women possess the fervor necessary to martyrs, but little of the balance needed for practical reconstructive work. Personally, I think it is entirely a matter of experience and education, for it is evident that women enter politics everywhere with great hesitancy. Even in America where equal suffrage has been a fact in some states for many years, we have only one or two women to point to as having attained political prominence.

Madame Kollontai possesses much charm. She is slim and pretty and vivacious. With a little too much the manner of a public speaker she talks so easily on any subject, even to reporters, that it almost gives an impression of insincerity. Her open mind is in reality an evidence of the kind of sincerity which has no fear of publicity. She likes Americans and knows more about this country than most Russians. But she has not always known. Some years ago, when lecturing here, she happened to be in Paterson during the great strike there. When she saw the workers marching through the streets, she rushed into a room full of people and exclaimed: "A revolution has begun!" Last year, in speaking of America, she said it was the country least agitated by revolutionary thought.

Like all enthusiastic Communists, she follows Lenin's lead in striving to westernize Russia. One day she very greatly surprised me by saying, "Why don't you write a series of articles about America? Write for Russia about America as you now write for America about Russia."

"What good will it do?" I asked.

"A great deal," she replied. "It is time Russia got acquainted with America. Because of the old censorship we never learned the value of reporters. And now that we are through forever with isolation, except when it is forced upon us, we ought to acquaint ourselves thoroughly with other countries. The women ought to know, for example, how American women got suffrage and what part women take in public affairs. We ought to know the status of the immigrants and of the Negroes, how you solve your unemployment problems, the status of farmers, of city workers, the percentage of wealth controlled by rich people. We ought to know about your schools and colleges. It ought to be explained to us just what the real difference is between the Republican and the Democratic Party and how much influence the Socialist Party has. Yes, there are a thousand things we ought to know."

I did not write the articles, but in explaining American ideas and institutions to Kollontai it somehow placed my country in a curious new light in my own eyes. I began to realize that things which have grown quite ordinary and familiar to us may appear entirely absurd and unreasonable to foreigners. Kollontai said that she hoped Russia would some day have reporters in America cabling home as busily as our reporters do from Russia. Russians, she thought, have in so many ways remained ridiculously provincial in spite of their ideas on internationalism.

Her feminist heart was deeply touched when I told her about a group of American women who had paraded on Fifth Avenue carrying signs of protest against the blockade. Tears came to her eyes. "You can't imagine," she said, "how much courage such a little act of sympathy gives us. What a pity that the story of those women is not known in Russia and not read by every peasant mother."

She was openly indignant about the stories circulated abroad that Russian women were *"nation-*

alized." When we first discussed this rumor she refused to believe that anybody in America could have seriously considered it, but when I explained about the Overman Committee and other official and semi-official affairs, she flew into a rage against the narrowness and prejudices of some of our statesmen. She claimed that the simplest peasant would not believe such indecent lies against American women. "Your senators," she said, "could very well have acquainted themselves with the real facts about our women, who have always taken such a glorious part in every movement for emancipation.

"American men," continued Madame Kollontai, "are known the world over as kind and chivalrous. But chivalry can be a little old-fashioned in this century. Certainly, there is much to criticize and much to improve in our new struggling republic. But have you ever thought how absurd it was that the very much pampered American woman was forced to picket the White House as part of a campaign for equal suffrage? And that for such acts she was sent to prison? It is more absurd also when you remember that at that very moment a Southern gentleman sat at the White House as President.

Naturally, such things appear inconsistent to us but we manage to see them in the right proportion. We know that in spite of these inconsistencies, Americans are a generous people, at heart friendly to Russia and the world."

Another time she said, "When our revolution came we obtained equality for everybody who was willing to work. Don't fail to comprehend what a stride that was! We didn't have to have a civil war to free the Tartars or the Turko-men as you did to free the Negro, and it certainly never was in anybody's mind, on any side, to disenfranchise Russian women, much less to nationalize them."

Nevertheless, Madame Kollontai finds even a revolutionary government can be run too largely by men. If it does nothing worse it has a very bad habit of overlooking women. But it cannot overlook them for long while Madame Kollontai is about, for she never fails to appear at the important congresses to remind the delegates of their sins; to goad them into discussions of women and women's problems.

"Women's congresses," she told me, "are absolutely necessary in the present state of development. And these congresses are not confined by any means to politics. I have been bringing peasant women to Moscow from all over Russia and we have told them how to take care of babies and how to prevent disease. We have also instructed them in local, national and international politics. A woman who has gone to Moscow from some remote village is more or less of a personality when she returns and you can be sure that her journey is an event to the whole village. She always goes back well supplied with literature and educational posters. She, naturally, stimulates an interest in the whole community in politics and hygiene, especially among the women. Such congresses are the only ones I know that have a far-reaching effect."

"I have been laughed at," she said, "because so far I have brought here only a few women from the harems of Turkestan. These women have thrown aside their veils. Everybody stares at them, they are a curiosity which gives the congresses a theatrical atmosphere. Yet all pioneering work is theatrical. It was distinctly theatrical when the audiences used to throw eggs at your pioneer suffragists. . . . How else would we get in touch wih Mohammedan women except through women?" How else, indeed? Other Russian educators have answered the question this way: Through Mohammedan men. It was by educating the Tartar men that the Tartar women became free. The Tartars are mostly all Mohammedans but their women no longer wear veils. Whereas the brave women Kollontai has induced to come to her congresses have been divorced by their husbands and have lost their homes and children.

Madame Kollontai's political judgment, even from the standpoint of an orthodox Communist, is often very bad. She has unlimited courage and on several occasions has openly opposed Lenin. As for Lenin, he has crushed her with his usual unruffled frankness. Yet in spite of her fiery enthusiasm she understands "party discipline" and takes defeat like a good soldier. If she had left the revolution four months after it began she could have rested forever on her laurels. She seized those rosy first moments of elation, just after the masses had captured the state, to incorporate into the Constitution laws for women which are far-reaching and unprecedented. And the Soviets are very proud of these laws which already have around them the halo of all things connected with the Constitution. It is almost impossible that that institution which came to life through her enthusiasm and determination will ever cease to be. The laws I refer to are particularly those in regard to expectant mothers, orphans, illegitimate children and the state care of maternity hospitals, known as Palaces of Motherhood.

Madame Kollontai is about fifty years of age and appears much younger. She has dark brown hair and blue eyes and could easily be taken for an American. She is one of the few women Communists who cares about her appearance. By that I do not mean that she enjoys any luxury. She lives in one room in a Soviet hotel. But she is pretty and knows how to wear her clothes. Once I complimented her on a smart little fur toque she was wearing. She laughed and said, "Yes, one must learn tricks in Russia, so I have made my hat out of the tail of my coat which is already five years old."

She comes from well-to-do middle-class parents and her first husband while not rich was, as an officer of the old régime, able to afford her a good deal of comfort. They had one child, a son. As a young girl Kollontai went to the best schools and after her marriage never ceased to study. She is an unusually gifted linguist, speaking eleven languages and often acting as official interpreter at the Soviet, as well as the International Congresses.

A curiously touching and disillusioning phase of the revolution was the Soviet Government's sincere attempt to wipe out prostitution from the young republic. In this fight Kollontai took and still takes a leading part. Way back in March, 1917, the infamous Yellow Tickets were destroyed. On the surface it appeared then as if the whole idea of traffic in women had forever ended. But even after the economic pressure was removed the curse returned. Angelica Balabonova, one of the most loved and honored of the women revolutionists as well as one of the most intellectual, wrote a stinging denunciation of what she called the "Soviet Barishnas." (Translated, Soviet Ladies.) The term soon came to be the most insulting phrase in the Russian language. It came to mean a woman who, in spite of everything, insisted on a life of shame.

So disgraceful do the Soviets regard this phase of Russian life that indignant citizens formed committees and raids took place. Women were arrested and thrown into concentration camps. And still the evil continued. At last the Central

Government took the problem in hand, as did the Central Organ of the Communist Party. Kollontai, writing on this matter, concludes: "The Women's Sections show lively and active interest in this matter since prostitution is a scourge which falls chiefly upon the women of the working class. This is our task, the task of the Women's Sections, to begin a general propaganda concerned with questions connected with prostitution, since it is in our interest to develop the revolution in the domain of the family and to stabilize relations between the sexes."

The government report is illuminating and shows above all else that the Soviet officials are not afraid to face facts, which is the first and best weapon of defense.

The Inter-departmental Commission makes the statement that, in Soviet Russia, prostitution appears in two forms:

1. In the form of professional prostitution.

2. In the form of secret earnings.

The first form is very slightly developed and is of slight extent. In Petrograd, for example, where raids were undertaken against prostitutes, this mode of combating prostitution practically yielded no results. The second form, although highly developed in other countries, also assumes a great variety of forms in Russia. Prostitution is practised by Soviet employees, in order to obtain for the sale of caresses, boots that go up to the knees; prostitution is resorted to by mothers of families, working women, peasant women, who are out after flour for their children and sell their bodies to the manager of the rations division in order to obtain from him a full bag of the precious flour. Sometimes the girls in the offices associate with their male superiors, not for manifestly material gain, for rations, shoes, etc., but in the hope of advancement in office. And there is an additional form of prostitution—"careerist prostitution"—which is also based in the last analysis on material gain.

The Commission made this recommendation after many hot debates: "All persons wandering in the streets and deserting their work should be assigned to the Commissariat of Social Welfare and thus sent out, in accordance with general fundamental considerations, either to the Sections for the Distribution of Labor Power of the People's Commissariat of Labor, or to courses, sanatoria, hospitals, and only after a repeated desertion by a prostitute, in other words, after a malicious effort to desert, should the individual be subjected to forced labor. There is no special culpability attached to prostitutes. They are in no way to be segregated from the other bodies of deserters from work. This is a revolutionary and important step, worthy of the first Workers' Republic of the world."

That such a liberal attitude is really effective is proven by the fact that in Soviet Russia to-day there is less prostitution than anywhere else in the world. Under the Tsar, Russia was known as the most disgraceful country in this respect. And Kollontai says, "There is no doubt that the poor, insufficient pay for female labor continues, in Soviet Russia, to serve as a chief factor. Under the law the earnings of men and women are equal, but the great majority of women are unskilled laborers. It resolves itself into a question of how to make female labor skilled labor. And the second case is the political backwardness of women. It is not the woman who is inspired and carried away by the idea of the revolution and the desire to aid reconstruction who falls into this pool of degradation."

In one of her pamphlets, Madame Kollontai declaims with pride: "By virtue of the decree of December 18, 1917, divorce has ceased to be a luxury accessible only to the rich." It has been interesting to watch the outcome of this decree through four years. Among the peasants divorce was practically unknown and still remains so. The city workers have not availed themselves of this "luxury" to any considerable degree. Whether Kollontai likes it or not, the only people who will continue to take advantage of such freedom will be the idle and the intellectuals. Divorces have little attraction for simple workers. Labor and poverty bring husband and wife closer to one another "for better or for worse."

Periodically, Kollontai attacks family life and claims that it is the only institution that Communists are afraid to reform. One needs only to look about at the leaders of the movement to wonder why they should be concerned in reforming it. Lenin leads a distinctly normal family life, as do Trotsky and Kalinin. The wives of these Commissars work and are interesting, well-known personalities. Kollontai herself is married. Her inconsistencies are her most feminine trait as well as one of her most alluring characteristics.

LEON TROTSKY, SOVIET WAR LORD

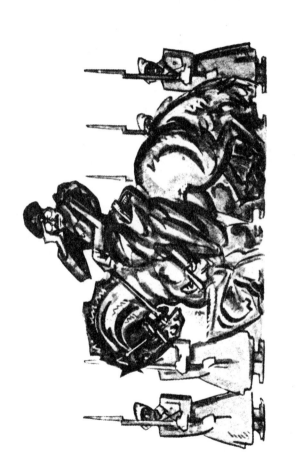

TROTSKY

LEON TROTSKY, SOVIET WAR LORD

MINISTER OF WAR, Leon Trotsky, has no prototype in history. Therefore, he cannot be compared, he can only be contrasted. He is without question the most dramatic character produced during the whole sweep of the Russian revolution and its only great organizer. No man will overshadow his eminence in the history of the revolution except Lenin. They will remain the two most distinguished personalities. They are complementary figures. Lenin represents thought; Trotsky represents action. Trotsky's genius might have burned itself out in some wild enthusiasm or some consuming rage if it had not been for the cooling influence of Lenin. On the other hand, Lenin's plans, no matter how carefully thought out, could not have materialized without the solid backing of Trotsky's bayonets.

Outside of Russia we are always hearing rumors of the conflict of these two personalities. We imagine Trotsky continually conspiring to usurp the place of Lenin; nothing could be further from the truth. Trotsky would consider the elimination of Lenin, through any cause, as the greatest calamity. He would not only think Russia had lost her wisest leader, but he would consider himself lost. He touched the very highest peak of revolutionary fervor when he made his famous speech in Moscow after Lenin had been shot and terribly wounded by an assassin and when small hope of recovery was entertained. "We will him to live and he will live!" he cried to an audience which rose to its feet in a wave of irrepressible emotion.

It was this speech which lighted the torch of the Red Terror as a back-fire against the White Terror, already so far under way that the very life of the revolution was at stake. But it is well for Trotsky and for the revolution that Trotsky did not direct this terror; he was too passionate and too thorough a soul to have been entrusted with such a conflagration.

Trotsky is not a diplomat. He was not successful as Foreign Minister. Diplomacy is too cut and dried to be harmonious with his talents. To be a good diplomat one must be contained and calculating and unemotional, content with the material on hand; one cannot be an originator. Trotsky is essentially an originator. It was not his destiny to accept the ready-made. It was his destiny to tear Russia out of old ruts and send her bleeding but inspired down new ways; it was his destiny to make war on Russian inertia, which is the curse of Russia and the whole East.

In Trotsky we discern something distinctly elemental. He looks like a fighter, with his burning eyes and sharp decisive way of speaking, his gestures, his quick regular gait. When he is calm he does not appear to be himself. But even in ordinary conversation he bestirs himself, he throw himself headlong into every discussion, and the listener is so carried away that he remembers it all afterward with astonishment. The storm Trotsky started in Russia, while it did not rage without wreckage, at least had the effect of waking up a nation out of its medieval slumber. Wherever he goes he stirs people, either individually or collectively. No one is neutral about him, Trotsky is either loved or despised.

In the Red Army, he has all the energetic young men of the nation assembled and under his influence. He has charge of their education. The majority have learned to read and write in his army schools. The way they express it is that he has given them "new eyes."

Trotsky is the idol of the Red Army. His amazing physical vigor combined with a very un-Russian orderliness, his personal bravery and reckless defiance of custom, make their former leaders appear dull and backward. He creates in his pupils a deep dissatisfaction for all that is old and outworn. These young men come from the villages, from every province in Russia. When they go back home they look at the village with disapproval, they want to change everything. In a little while, because of their superior knowledge they become men of importance, leading their local Soviets and attending the Congresses in Moscow.

If Trotsky can not understand the little ridiculous points of diplomatic etiquette, the cunning and sensitiveness which mark a good diplomat, he thoroughly comprehends how to take advantage of every modern appliance and every modern method of running the War Office. No War Office under any Tsar could boast such order as Trotsky's. Everything goes like clock-work, you are aware of energy and efficiency; it has the hum of a high-power engine.

The young aides in Trotsky's office are as smart as in the French War Office. He has a way of attracting venturesome youth from everywhere. His pet school, which is the Military Academy in Moscow, where the General Staff men are trained, is full of these soldiers-of-fortune. I was invited to an entertainment there one evening by a young Lieutenant-Colonel. This man was the son of a rich Swedish banker and he was but twenty-six years old. He introduced me to a number of other foreigners, young men like himself, who had risen to high ranks through many desperate campaigns. "We have every nation represented here but America," said a Bulgarian. I do not know whether these men were Communists or how loyal they felt to that cause, but they were willing to follow Trotsky to their graves.

A visit to this academy gives one quite a clear idea of how the former classes in Russian society are amalgamating under the new order. It is full of the sons of the bourgeoisie. And the professors are almost without exception the old professors who taught in these schools under the Tsar. Men like Brusilov, who is a Russian patriot and would defend his government under any régime against outsiders, have enormous prestige. As the White Generals went down to defeat one after the other, the young men even of conservative parents came to believe that if they could not swallow the Communist formulas whole, they could, at least, remain loyal Russians. And once in the military schools, they fell under the influence of revolutionary soldiers. Being young and full of Slavic idealism, they often capitulated and in such cases were rapidly promoted. In the Kronstadt day the young men of this type were more concerned than any of the others, perhaps because if the Red Army were to be defeated, they would be the first to be killed by the opposition. When General Brusilov's only son was captured in Siberia by the White Forces, he was executed simply because he was the son of Brusilov.

Trotsky believes in peace. He has told me this almost every time I talked with him, but he is, nevertheless, an apostle of force. "The happiest moment of my life," he said, "was when I thought I could turn the Red Army into a Labor Army to reconstruct Russia." Trotsky would probably have been very successful with his Labor Army, provided he could have kept it really an army, with army rules and discipline. An army is Trotsky's perfect medium for work. He likes a Labor Army better than a fighting army because it makes him happier to build than to destroy.

TROTSKY

But all his organizing genius goes for nothing if he cannot have order and discipline.

About three years ago Lenin appointed Trotsky Minister of Railways in addition to his post as War Minister. Trotsky took a trip over the country and found transportation generally smashed and the railway employees as lacking in morale as he had once found the Russian soldiers. He immediately began to re-build transportation with every atom of his strength. If a train was not on time, there had to be a reason given, which had ceased to be done in those days. In fact, no one was ever deeply concerned about exact arrivals and departures of trains under any régime. The Trans-Siberian Railway was the only efficient road which ever operated in Russia. But Trotsky began to make such an everlasting row about these matters that the railway men were aghast. There had always been graft and laziness and indifference, they had no doubt that there always would be, even under government control. Trotsky hauled them up, threatened them with imprisonment and even with death. The result was that the unions were so roused that they threatened a general strike. The situation grew worse and worse. Finally Lenin, to avert a national crisis, dismissed Trotsky and wrote an open letter to the unions about it and Trotsky showed his real fineness of character by accepting his defeat in silence. And yet if he had been in charge of the roads they would certainly not be in the condition that they now are and many thousands of lives in the famine area would have been saved.

Trotsky cannot bear Russian slothfulness and he is constantly irritated by Russian indifference to sanitation. He insists on the utmost fastidiousness and neatness for all who work with him. An amusing scandal took place in Moscow at the time of one of the International Conventions. Trotsky had instructed a Red Army physician to inspect the hotel in which the foreign delegates were to stay and report if it was in order. The physician merely went down to the building and finding a fine grand piano there, whiled his time away playing and let the inspection go. In due course of time the delegates arrived and the first night they were all routed out of bed by insects. This came to the ears of Trotsky and he was so furiously angry that he had the doctor arrested and announced that he would have him shot. The delegates flew around in a fine state of excitement with a petition which they all signed begging

Trotsky to spare the physician's life. As a matter of fact Trotsky would not have shot him, but his threats are reminiscent of the day of Tsar Peter who found it necessary to shoot a number of nobles before the others would shorten their long coats as he had ordered by royal decree.

Trotsky is a student of the French Revolution. He lived a long time in France and he loves France, in spite of its hostility to Soviet Russia. Some of his closest friends are Frenchmen who knew him in Paris and who followed him to Russia and work with him there. He never forgets his friends and has a real capacity for permanent friendships. Russians are, as a rule, very changeable in their personal relationships but one can depend on Trotsky.

As an orator he reminds one much more of the French revolutionary orators. Russians speak more slowly and more logically and with less fire. Trotsky stirs his audiences by his own force and by striking phrases. There were times when these splendid literary phrases infuriated Lenin; from the public platform he once called Trotsky a "phrase-maker." But this was way back in the Smolny days when Trotsky was more untamed than he is now, and before Lenin realized that Trotsky would be his most able assistant.

While Trotsky was in America he was the editor of a Russian newspaper and apparently caught the American feeling for on-the-minute news. He is the easiest official to interview in Moscow and entirely the most satisfactory, because he is free from the general reticence and distrust of the press which most of the Commissars have. I once wrote him a note saying that I was writing a story about the Red Army and would like some material. The very same day he sent me down a great sack of copy. There were many Red Army magazines and newspapers that I had never heard of. There were handbooks and statistics and maps and, besides all that, there was a permission to go to any of the fronts and to attend any of the lectures at the various schools.

One of the most important departments of the Red Army is that known as the Political-Cultural. A report is made daily by this Department concerning the morale of the soldiers and the relation between the army and the civilian population. This Department conducts the classes in reading and writing and elementary technical training and vocational training; the work is carried on even in fighting days and right up to the front.

The soldiers are also taught to be interested in physical culture and have been learning games like Rugby. There was a good deal of excitement in the Red Army when a Russian team beat a team composed of foreign delegates to the Third Congress of the International in Moscow.

Soldiers are urged to attend the Art Galleries and the theatres. Art exhibitions and lectures on art take place in the soldiers' clubs. Here also they often build and act their own plays; most of these are about the revolution and will no doubt gradually settle down into national patriotic epics.

It is hard to know whether Trotsky will ever have another chance to experiment as he would like with his Labor Army, but that is his ambition. Lenin's opinion is that it is absolutely an experiment which can work out only if the men themselves are willing to submit to this plan for the good of Russia. Men never do efficient work if they do not want to, Lenin believes. Trotsky answers this argument by saying, "But we have the advantage over the rest of the world in that respect; we can try any schemes we please and if they do not work, we can change our minds."

His plan for a Labor Army I have taken from notes and I quote Trotsky's exact words:

"Russia is an industrially undeveloped country; and our economic apparatus is ruined by six years of war and revolution. We must be able to concentrate labor upon certain emergency tasks—where it is most necessary. For example, the Ural mining district needs fifty thousand skilled workers, two hundred thousand semi-skilled and two hundred thousand laborers. We should be able to send these workers where they are most needed; of course, this would be done in co-operation and after consultation with the Unions and Shop Committees."

His idea of maintaining the regular fighting force is to have it on a very much smaller scale. "Russia is now being redistricted. The new districts will be ordered according to their economic character, as economic units. Each district will be the headquarters of a division whose task is to mobilize the population not only for the army but for the work.

"The army divisions on the frontiers are to be constantly renewed. Each will remain on duty for three or four months, and then be sent home to work. In this way the whole male population will be trained to arms, each knowing his place in his regiment, and also his proper work."

In the brief period before the Polish offensive, the Labor Army had been started full blast and at that time it had the approval of the army and the unions. Perhaps in another half year it will again be working. It is interesting to know how they managed. I will give one example. In six weeks the Labor Army built the great steel bridge over the Kam River, blown up by Kolchak. Thus the direct route to Siberia was restored. They restored the railway at Yamburg. They cut millions of feet of fire-wood for the cities. They were making such progress that if the Polish offensive had never taken place, the cities would actually have been provisioned and provided with wood before the first snow of that year.

One can make vast speculation about Trotsky. He is the sort of man who, if he is given full power in a great plan of this kind, will work miracles, but if he is hampered by petty labor disputes and a thousand petty jealousies, will fail utterly. I always have believed that if he had been interested in finance instead of social revolution he would now be our greatest banker. If he had been interested in the war from the Allied standpoint he would have been a great military hero.

Trotsky was born in 1877. He is the son of a colonist of Jewish faith from the government of Kherson near Elizabethgrad. He was indicted in a judicial investigation of the Workman's Syndicate of South Russia in 1898 and sentenced to Siberia for four years. He settled in the city of Verkholensk and later escaped. He became president of the Soviet of Workmen's Deputies in Petrograd in 1905. For activities in that organization he was sent again into exile to Tobolsk and again escaped. After that he lived in Paris and Vienna and later in the United States. He returned to Russia after the beginning of the revolution. Trotsky has a wife and two children. His wife is young and excessively good looking and is interested in revolutionary activities. Trotsky, like Lenin, is very proud of his wife.

Trotsky might never have written his name as indelibly as he has on the page of history if it had not been for the peculiar circumstances of the war. His heroic strivings might have been spent aimlessly, if chance had not thrust into his hands the task of rebuilding an army. And no man can

build a great army out of a rabble and not be famous. Many points were in his favor beside cir-
cumstance. He might not have found even his
genius or his vitality enough to meet world opposition without the use of trained officers, men who
were willing to submerge their own opinions for
the moment in order to save Russia. A day will
come perhaps when General Brusilov's words will
be known to all Russian school children as the
words of Patrick Henry are known to American
children. This was his advice to all classes of Russians during intervention and the blockade:

"When a steamer on the boundless ocean is in
danger, it is not a time for starting quarrels as
to this principle or that, or to seek the numerous
causes for the fact that our ship of state may have
merged into an unfavorable sea, but it is our duty
to exert immediately all our thoughts and forces
to save the vessel from destruction and bring her
back to port with the smallest possible loss."

I saw Trotsky again this summer (the summer
of 1922) and asked him what he had done about
reducing the army. Of course, because of the new
economic policy, a Labor Army was out of the
question. He told me that he had reduced the army
from 5,300,000 to 800,000, including the navy. A

greater reduction than that, he said, was impossible.

"We stand always ready to reduce our army," said Trotsky, "even to liquidating it fully, whenever our closest and our farthest neighbors accept a program of disarmament. In January we offered disarmament. Europe refused even the suggestion. Later we asked our close neighbors, with the same result. If America would only take the initiative in this respect," he shrugged and smiled, "well, we would support her with our whole heart."

ENVER PASHA

AND THE

MOHAMMEDANS

ENVER PASHA

ENVER PASHA
AND THE
MOHAMMEDANS

No man I ever met lives so completely in the immediate moment as Enver Pasha; the past he puts behind him, the future he leaves to Allah. His only hero is Napoleon. In Moscow he was the *avant coureur* of the new understanding between Russia and the Mohammedan world, which means Turkey, Afghanistan, Persia, Bokhara and enough of India to shake the British Empire.

Any man who has brains and gives all his being to the task in hand is bound to possess personality and power and, very likely, charm. Enver Pasha certainly has charm, in spite of his very obvious opportunism, and the cruelty and lack of conscience which a fatalistic belief inspires. Interested in himself above all things, he is a curious contrast to those men who are trying to blot out individualism and make the state all-important.

As far as there was any social life in Moscow,

Enver was, for the nonce, the social lion. Some future historian will probably call him the Don Juan of the revolution, though it is only fair to say that he resisted this alluring doom with an uncomplimentary coldness; he was too absorbed in politics to be interested in social conquest. The real reason for the shower of attention bestowed on him by the ladies of Moscow was the natural reaction of those ladies to a life almost unendurably monotonous and difficult.

There was something very pitiful about the way actresses smiled at Enver across the footlights and unearthed old pictures of him in his elaborate War Minister regalia, when he still wore the "Kaiser" moustache, the gold braid and numerous medals. One evening we went to the dressing room of a prima donna where we were invited for tea during an intermission. Enver sat stiffly in his chair, refusing to talk, but his uncle, Halil Pasha, the former Commander of the Mesopotamian and Caucasian fronts, caused much merriment by fighting a sham duel with wooden swords. His opponent was a singer dressed as a medieval knight.

Besides the actresses several of the old aristocracy were gracious to Enver and even the pretty wife of a Commissar attached to the Foreign Office wrote him what would have been considered an intriguing note, in another time and place. She offered to teach him Russian if he would teach her French and he replied curtly that he was not a "professor."

But Enver was not always over-serious and unbending. In a certain small circle of friends he was quite otherwise. And circumstances, which so largely decide our destinies, gave me an opportunity to know him as well as one alien to his religion could know him. He was allotted by the Foreign Office quarters in the little palace where I was living. For half a year I saw him every day, sat next to him at table and occasionally we went to the theatres and the Turkish Embassy. During that time Enver told me a great deal about his life and his ambitions.

He had known my husband in Constantinople, and was away from Moscow at the time of my husband's death. As soon as he returned he called on me, bringing Halil and the Turkish Ambassador, Ali Fued Pasha, with him. All three were extremely kind and sympathetic. From that moment until I left Moscow the Turks did everything possible to make life less tragic for me, and I gained an insight into the Turkish character which I had never imagined. The Turks have a peculiar capacity for friendship. And friendship, once given, has no bournes; a friend is a friend through everything — sorrow, dishonor, poverty, as well as wealth and success. An enemy, on the other hand, is beyond all consideration; he is spared nothing, forgiven nothing.

Enver has the personal vanity of the enthusiast and he imagines that everything he does he does well. The only way to cope with his conceit is to be brutally frank. I discovered early in our acquaintance that frankness by no means offends him. One of Enver's nicest qualities is that he likes to discover his faults as well as his virtues; he is eager to improve himself.

He has a passion for making pencil sketches of people he meets and always goes about with a pencil and a pad of paper in his pocket. In the house where we lived he made sketches of all the guests and all the servants. He made, in all, six very uninteresting portraits of me. One morning when the tea was more tasteless than ever and the bread especially sour and muddy so that I felt I could not manage to eat a single bite, I could not help feeling unpleasantly resentful to see Enver busy with his sketches and full of enthusiasm. And while I sat staring at the terrible meal, he proceeded to make a life-size portrait of me which was incredibly bad. I remember that I wondered where on earth he ever got such a large piece of paper in Russia. When he had finished the sketch he signed his name with a flourish and presented it to me. I took it but said nothing. Enver has the curiosity of a child, and, after a long silence, he asked me if it was possible that I did not really like it. I said that I thought he had no talent for drawing. He became suddenly quite angry and said in a low voice, "But do you realize I have signed my name to it?"

"Your name doesn't mean anything on a picture," I explained. "If it was an order for an execution or an advance it would be another matter. You can't make a good drawing just by signing your name to it."

He frowned and then grew cordial as suddenly as he had grown angry. He rose and bowed to me in a most courtly way. "You can't imagine," he said, "how pleasing arrogance is to me." His three dominating characteristics being bravery, hauteur and recklessness, he imagined that these motives also guided the actions of his friends.

Enver never seemed to be able to loaf in the easy manner of most Orientals. His mental and physical vitality is more like that of an enthusiastic and healthy American. Every morning he rose early to go for a long walk, he read a great deal, took at least three lessons in some foreign language every week and was constantly writing articles for Turkish papers which he printed on a hand press in his own room, and he held almost daily conferences either with the Russians or the Mohammedans. He does not drink or smoke and is devoutly religious.

He likes any discussion which reveals another person's deepest emotions. If he cannot rouse one any other way he does so by some antagonistic remark which often he does not mean at all. For example, he is extremely liberal in his opinions about women and does not think they should be excluded from political life. Nevertheless, he said to a young actress at tea one afternoon in my apartment, when they were talking about woman suffrage, that she would be better off in a harem. Being an ardent feminist, she rose and fairly shouted at him: "Enver Pasha, you may be a great man in the East, but just listen to me! I am one of the first actresses of my profession. In my

world it is every bit as great and important for me
to remain an actress as it is for you in your world
to remain a warrior or a diplomat."

Enver took his scolding in very good humor.
Afterwards he told me that he had never liked this
actress before. "Independence is a great thing in
women. Our women lack it and many of them
are just puppets on this account."

He was always extremely interested in American ideas and American opinions. He said he
could never understand why Americans were so
sentimental about Armenians. "Do they imagine
that Armenians never kill Turks? That is indeed
irony."

At the table he used to ask Mr. Vanderlip
questions about his proposed Kamchatka concessions. Vanderlip, like many Californians, is
rather violently anti-Japanese. His idea of having a naval base at Kamchatka amused Enver.
He said Vanderlip was killing two birds with one
stone, that he wished to manœuver the American
Government into a war with Japan, prove himself
a patriot, and at the same time protect his own
interests and grow rich. "So that," said Enver,
"if it really came about—the next war would be

for Vanderlip and should be known as 'Vanderlip's War.' "

When I asked, "Would you be sorry to see America and Japan at war?" he replied, "Not if England was involved. Anything which tends to draw England's attention away from us or which weakens the great powers, naturally gives Turkey a better chance for reconstruction. You understand that I'm not saying I want to see another war; I am simply saying that if those nations interested in destroying Turkey are occupied elsewhere it relieves us of war burdens and gives us a chance to carry out our own destinies."

He tried to get Mr. Vanderlip's reaction on women by the same tactics he employed with the actress. One day he said, "I have three wives and I'm looking for another." This was not true, but Mr. Vanderlip proved entirely gullible. "Good heavens," he said, regarding Enver in shocked surprise, "we Anglo-Saxons consider one wife enough tyranny. . . ."

"Naturally," Enver conceded, suavely, "with one there must be tyranny but with three or four or a hundred. . . . Ah, you must agree that is quite a different matter."

His sudden appearance in Moscow during the

blackest days of the blockade as well as the blackest days for the Central Powers proves him an incomparable soldier-of-fortune. With two suits of clothes, a pair of boots, a good revolver and a young German mechanician whom he could trust, he started by aeroplane from Berlin to Moscow. The story of how they had to land because of engine trouble near Riga, of how he was captured and spent two months in the Riga jail just at the moment when the whole Allied world was calling loudest for his blood, will remain a story which will have scanty advertisement from those British Secret Service men who like so well to turn journalists and write their own brave autobiographies.

Enver sat in the Riga jail as plain "Mr. Altman" who could not speak anything but German. He was scrutinized by every Secret Service man in the vicinity and pronounced unanimously a Jewish German Communist of no importance. By appearing humble, inoffensive and pleasant, he soon worked his way into the confidence of the warden, was released and escaped to Moscow. He arrived just in time to rush off for the dramatic Baku conference.

The Communists understood perfectly well that

Enver Pasha was not at the Oriental Conference as a sudden and sincere convert to Internationalism, and he knew that they knew. Both Zinoviev and Enver were actors taking the leading rôles in a significant historical pageant. The results are really all that matter, since the motives will soon be forgotten.

When Enver turned to Moscow he had no other place to turn to and when Zinoviev took him to Baku, Zinoviev knew no other means of effectively threatening the English in order to change their attitude on the blockade. Zinoviev could not complain about Enver's shallow attitude towards Socialism since there was hardly anything Socialistic about Zinoviev's appeal for a "holy war." Enver summed up his feelings about the new alliance thus: "For the future of Turkey and the future of the East a friendship with Russia is worth more to the Turks than any number of military victories. And we have to build that friendship while we have the opportunity."

His way of living without any regrets and as if there were no to-morrows is rather startling at times. I remember when Talaat Pasha, his lifelong friend, was murdered by an Armenian in Berlin, he read the message with no show of emotion

and his only comment was: "His time had come!"
But against an excessive temptation on the part of
fate to record Enver's death prematurely, in his
own words, he "sleeps with one eye open," carries
a dagger and a loaded automatic. Once when we
talked about the possibility of his being assassinated he said, "I have been near death so many
times that these days I live now seem to be a sort
of present to me."

Enver is no open sesame to those who do not
know him well. He really has the traditional
Oriental inscrutability. The first two or three
times I talked with him, we stumbled along rather
lamely in French. Someone suggested to me that
he probably spoke several languages which, for
some unknown reason, he would not admit. So one
day I said abruptly, "Oh, let's speak English." He
looked at me with one of his sudden, rare smiles
and answered in my own language, "Very well,
if you prefer it."

When I asked him how he learned English he
told me he had learned it from an English spy.
"He came to me as a valet and professed deep love
for Turkey. For several months we studied diligently. One day I thought I would test his love

for Turkey so I ordered him to the front. He was killed. Later, we found his papers."

"Were you surprised?" I asked him.

"Why, not at all," said Enver. "He really showed a great deal of pluck. The only thing I had against him was that he taught me a lot of expressions not used at court."

"Like what?"

"Like 'don't mention it,'" said Enver, laughing. "And the terrible thing about learning such an expression," he said, "is that it is so sharp and so definite and often fits an occasion so aptly that it flashes in one's mind and can't be forgotten. American slang is extremely picturesque and expressive, but it is not dignified enough to be used by diplomats."

Everyone is familiar with Enver's "direct action" method of playing politics. One of the ways he was wont to remove troublesome rivals in the days of the Young Turk Revolution was to go out and shoot them with his own hand. This "impulsiveness" got him into grave trouble with the Soviets in spite of all his sensible utterances to the contrary. When he was "shifted" to Bokhara so that he would not be in the way of either Kemal or the Russians, he got bored and started a war of his own. One night he fled into the hills of Afghanistan and soon began to gather recruits around him. A few nights after that one of the principal officials of the Bokharan Republic also fled to join Enver. This performance was repeated until over half the Bokharan cabinet had fled. Then fighting began and we got vague rumors of battles, but only through the Soviet press.

In August, 1922, we heard that Enver had been killed, that his body had been found on the field of battle. There was even romance surrounding him and his supposed death. Stories were circulated that when the body was picked up and examined, the letters of an American girl were found next his heart. I went to see Jacob Peters, who has charge now of all the Eastern Territory and who was then in Moscow. He laughed heartily and said he would show me the "information." It consisted of three very hazy telegrams which had been three weeks on the way. The men who sent the telegrams and discovered the body had never seen Enver. There was no mention of letters. And Peter's opinion of the whole affair was that there was nothing at all authentic in the story or else it was "a trick of Enver's to sham being dead."

Peters' theory proved true. Within a few days fighting began again and Enver began to win.

He had conceived the notion of uniting all Turkestan and Bokhara and Keiva to the Angora government. It places the Soviets in a strange position. They may have to give in to him, though he will not actually be an "enemy," because neither the Turks nor the Russians can afford to break their treaty. Therefore, his private war in the south embarrasses the Soviets much more than it does Kemal, who needs only to disavow any connection with it, as do all the Turkish officials. If Enver wins he will add a nice slice to Turkish territory; if he loses, Turkey will be in the same position as before.

Enver, while he will always maintain a great prestige in the Mussulman world, will never oust Kemal. Mustapha Kemal Pasha is the great popular hero of a victorious Turkey, which but for him might never have even survived. There were times in the past when Enver was more important than Kemal, but that can never happen again in Kemal's life. Both men rose from the ranks and both are the sons of peasants. And Kemal at this moment is more important than the

Sultan. Greater than that no man can be under the banners of Mohammed.

One can hardly over-estimate the importance of the new Mohammedan unity, that new patriotic energy which has taken the place of the former lethargy and which already reaches out far beyond the borderland of the Faithful. The Mussulman world is reviving after a long sleep. And not only Mohammedans are uniting but the entire East and Middle East. Aside from Japan, a significant harmony is rapidly taking place, a harmony which evolves itself into a tremendous power. This power may decide the world's destiny before another generation.

Enver and Kemal Pasha, being aware of the purport of beginning that great concord by interwoven treaties with Russia, read the stars well. There must come a day also when that great sleeping giant, China, will be part of this alliance. And the seeds of that friendship have also been planted. The Chinese official delegations which came to Moscow were not only well received by the Russians, but they hob-nobbed with the Mohammedans like brothers.

TIKON AND THE RUSSIAN CHURCH

TIKON AND THE RUSSIAN CHURCH

THERE are two points of importance in regard to the Greek Orthodox Church and the Russian revolution. First, that the church has maintained itself and second, that it has issued no frantic appeals for outside help. While certain priests have allied themselves with counter-revolutionists, officially the church has never taken sides. Even at the present moment when a bitter conflict is on, the quarrel remains a family quarrel.

Tikon, the Patriarch, by remaining unruffled through the barricade and blockade days, proved himself a strong leader in a time when only strong leaders could survive. If he had been frightened or hostile in the Denikin or Kolchak days he might have shared the fate of the Romanoffs; if he had taken part in counter-revolutions, the church itself might have been badly shattered. But until recently, Tikon has been as placid as his ikons and as interested in the great change going on about him as a scientist. And therein lay his strength.

"Don't let any one pity me," he said last winter when I talked to him, "I am having the most interesting time of my life."

Much nonsense has been written about anti-church propaganda in Soviet Russia. Dozens of writers have discussed a certain rather obscure sign in Moscow which reads: "Religion is the opiate of the people." This sign, about three feet across, is painted high up on the north side of the Historical Museum building near the entrance to the Red Square. No one in Russia seems to be much interested in it and certainly it attracts less attention than any one of our million billboard advertisements. I tried for a year to find out who had put it up and what group it represented, but could never discover. It was a cab driver who said the wisest thing concerning it. "If somebody took it down," he said dryly, when I asked him what he thought of it, "no one would notice."

The anti-clerical posters gotten out at the beginning of the revolution, however, had a much more far-reaching influence. They were usually to the effect that the priests were hoarding the church lands and at the same time expecting the peasants to support them. Any idea which sanctions giving the land to the peasants is popular in Russia. It was not long before the peasants had seized the church lands and divided them through their land committees. But this did not make them atheists.

I remember meeting an old peasant leader from Siberia who had led a successful revolt against Kolchak. He was received as a hero when he arrived at Moscow for an All Russian Congress of Soviets. He told me a story about a priest in his community who was a counter-revolutionist. He said, "It usually is this way with me and with many of the peasants, we love God and we are religious but we hate the priests." I asked him if it was not possible to find good priests, and he began to tell me about one priest who had been very noble and self-sacrificing. But this was the only one he could think of. "The others disgrace God," he said.

And that is just what one must understand in order to comprehend the Russian church and its present position. The Soviets did not destroy the church or ruin it in any way—no outside pressure could do that. It was Rasputin and other "disgracers" who at last outraged even the credulous and easy-going peasants.

A revolution had to take place in the church as well as outside of it to save it at all. The church, at the time of the revolution, was as corrupt as the Tsardom. Nothing is better evidence of this than the way it was deserted by hundreds of priests as soon as the life in the monasteries ceased to be easy. Long before the upheaval the priesthood had grown dissolute. All that the revolution did was to give the church a pruning which saved its soul. By shearing it of its old luxuries it cut off the parasitic priests and by severing it from the state it took the church out of politics. It was forced to stand or fall by its own merits.

And when the wealth of the church was reduced to a certain point it became necessary for a priest to be such a good priest and so well loved and appreciated by his flock that his flock was willing to support him, in spite of the hard life and the terrible conditions. Thus a new and better clergy came into being.

The final test of the priesthood, however, came with the famine. All that was left of the church wealth, outside of the churches themselves, were the jewels in the ikons and the silver and gold ornaments which glitter in the shrines throughout Russia. The government decided to requisition these treasures. The priests who had been shriven in the revolutionary fire were glad and willing to part with these things, but there were many who resisted. The outcome was a split in the church ranks, as well as riots, intrigue, and bad feeling. There probably was a good deal of mismanagement on the part of a few arbitrary Soviet officials like Zinoviev, who do not seem to comprehend the sensitiveness of religious people and how easily outraged they are by outside intrusion. There is little doubt that this heightened a delicate and unfortunate situation. If a Church Committee had been allowed to select and turn over the jewels and precious metal, Tikon and other churchmen would probably never have been brought to trial.

However, the trials themselves are intensely interesting and mark an epoch in the life of the revolution. They actually mark the real beginning of public opinion in Russia and that, in any case, is a healthy development. It is like letting fresh air into a long-closed room. Discussions of the government and the church have for five years been going on in whispers behind closed doors. It now comes down to this: if the government is wrong and is unjustly stripping the church of wealth, the government will suffer by lack of support or even open hostility on the part of the peasants, who have so much power now that they can no longer be ignored on any question; and if the priests are wrong and prove themselves selfish in this time of need, the priests will be deposed. But the church itself will go on because the peasants are religious; they will continue to "love God" in the traditional manner.

About a week ago I met a Russian priest in New York and I asked him at once how he felt about the requisitioning of the jewels. He raised his hands devoutly. "What man could pray to God and hoard jewels at such a time?" he exclaimed. Then he showed me a very old and precious carved wooden cross. "There was a ruby in this cross," he said. "It was the only valuable thing I possessed. I can't tell you how happy I was when it was sold and the money used for relief. This is not a stone you see in it now; it is a piece of red glass, but it is somehow more precious to me than the ruby." Here is the expression of a really devout man and the only sort of priest that people will follow in such a crisis.

It is perfectly true that the leaders of the Communist movement are not religious. All students, in fact the entire "intelligentsia" or educated classes of Russia, were never religious. Before the revolution all groups of revolutionaries and literary folk prided themselves on their lack of religion. So anti-religion is not confined strictly to the leaders of the Communist movement. Any other party except the Monarchist Party would be equally devoid of interest in religion.

The Monarchists necessarily support the church because the Tsar was really head of the church. This has been true since the time of Peter the Great, who while not actually abolishing the office of Patriarch, never allowed another Patriarch to be elected. One of the curious and interesting sidelights of the revolution was that a few weeks after the church was separated ·from the state, a Patriarch was elected for the first time in two hundred years, so that while in one way the church lost its power, in another way it really came into its own.

Freedom of religion, as we know it in the United States, was a surprise and a shock to the members of the Russian church, for up until 1917 no other sects but the Greek Orthodox were permitted by law in Russia. Naturally, when other religious orders began to send in missionaries the old church protested, and when the Soviets answered that freedom of religion was now an established fact they did not understand it as "freedom" and called it discrimination. And it seemed like discrimination, because, while the Orthodox Church was losing its former possessions, other religions were gaining concessions.

Tikon, whose official title is Patriarch of Moscow and All the Russias, and who is called, with a sharp flavor of French revolutionary days, by the Supreme Revolutionary Tribunal, "Citizen Basil Ivanovitch Baliavin," was born in Pskoff in 1860. He was educated in Petrograd Theological Academy and became a monk upon the completion of his studies. He later held several important posts as a professor in theological institutions. He was consecrated Bishop of the Aleutian Isles and North America in 1897 and then came to America. In 1905 he was made Archbishop and moved the cathedral residence from San Francisco to New York. He returned to Russia in February, 1907, having been appointed Archbishop of Jaroslav. In 1913 he became Archbishop of Vilna. Early in 1917 he was elected Metropolitan of Moscow and in November of that same year, just when the Bolsheviks came into power, he became Patriarch.

Just what influenced Tikon and made him so

much more democratic than most of his colleagues, I do not know. My own opinion, after a conversation with him, is that he is somewhat of a student of history and a philosopher, as well as a priest. It is the opinion of many people, inside and outside of Russia, that it was his long residence in America which made him so liberal. Of one thing I feel sure. He would have resisted the Soviet Government if he had believed that it was better for the future of the church. I do not think he refrained because of any personal fears, but because he actually saw a real revival of religion in the fire through which the church was passing.

No one could have expected the church to embrace the revolution. The nobility and the clergy had walked too many centuries hand in hand. The nobility perished in the course of events and the church survived, as it did in France. And the church will continue to survive—merely the poorer by a few jewels or a few thousand acres of land. But it will never wield the same power that it once did or that it could wield if there was a return to Tsardom. It cannot be as strong, for example, as the Church of Rome is in Italy.

The real menace to the power of the Russian church lies in its own medieval outlook on life.

It has scarcely anything to do with anti-church propagandists or with opposition by force or by requisition. The youth of Russia is interested in reconstruction and the government for the first time. The young people have learned to read and to think. They are no longer content with the old forms; they are repelled by dissolute or un-Christ-like priests. If the church wishes to be strong and to have an influence in the life of the nation it cannot gain that influence by haggling over a pile of rubies and diamonds and emeralds while thousands of children are dying of hunger. The old peasants might follow Tikon when he says that the famine is the business of God, but the young people will not. It is almost inconceivable that a man can follow the lowly Christ in such a proud way. Certainly, the young Russians, who have so passionately defended the revolution, will never be satisfied with such a conception.

It seems very sad, from the religious point of view, that Tikon, who steered his church through the long period of fighting and destruction, should lose his equilibrium in the period of adjustment. He was able to smile through all the worst days of terror and suspicion. He could joke about the Cheka guard outside his door, he could calm his agitated congregations, but he could not sacrifice form. When I interviewed him he wore a gorgeous robe and jewels.

Tikon is sincere. Even in his clinging to the splendor of gold and jewels, he is sincere. It is his particular mystical way of loving God, which is difficult to understand in our age of materialism. Tikon, in a lesser degree, has many of those qualities of Lenin which make him a leader of men. If he had been as great a man as Lenin he would have thoroughly purified the church and led a great religious revival in Russia.

TCHICHERIN,
COMMISSAR FOR FOREIGN AFFAIRS,
AND HIS SUBORDINATES.

GREGORY VASSILIEVITCH TCHICHERIN

MAXIM LITVINOV, ASSISTANT COMMISSAR

LEONID KRASSIN

DAVID ROTHSTEIN

GREGORY WEINSTEIN

MICHAEL KARAKHAN

MR. FLORINSKY

MR. AXIONOV

GREGORY VASSILIEVITCH TCHICHERIN

MY FIRST interview with Tchicherin was at midnight and my last interview was at five in the morning. This happens to cover a fairly complete rotation of the official hours of the Soviet Foreign Office.

One evening at a box party in the Bolshoi Theatre, Enver Pasha remarked: "I have to kill time somehow for three hours after the play. Halil Pasha and I have an appointment with Mr. Tchicherin at two o'clock." In spite of his smiling Oriental inscrutability and a palpable diplomatic duty to conform to everything Russian, one could feel an amused disapproval of such official unconventionality.

This eccentric habit of turning night into day, with every floor of the Foreign Office blazing like a lighthouse in a city which by municipal decree is put to bed before midnight in order to save fuel, naturally creates an almost fantastic air of whimsicality. Mr. Tchicherin makes no excuse for this "vice," as one of his secretaries very cleverly phrased it; he simply finds night more harmonious for his tasks than day and with that lack of consideration which dreamers always consciously or unconsciously assume, he forces his whole staff to follow his example. The result is that his clerks make a mad scramble to get transferred into another government department.

Everything about Tchicherin is as consistently contrary to an ordered life as his inversion of working hours. Born an aristocrat, trained under the Tsar for the diplomatic service, delicate, cultured, aloof, with a fine gesture of Quixotic generosity, he has thrown his life and his fortunes in with the cause of the proletariat with all the abandon of religious fervor.

His aloofness is so evident that one can hardly find any concordance about the astounding decision of such an obvious æsthete to become an active part of revolution—which is sweat and blood and violence. Perhaps that explains why he wraps his vision round him like a cloak and shuts out the sun in order not to be disturbed and disillusioned by reality. We were all brought up on stories about kings who were gay-fellows-well-met and could outdance and outdrink their soldiers; on nobles who turned out to be Robin Hoods. But, alas, who can imagine Tchicherin rollicking at a workers' picnic or smoking a friendly pipe with a Red soldier?

No simple person will ever feel intimate or at home with his super-class indifference to material surroundings. A scrubwoman is just as uncomfortable in his presence as was the intrepid Mrs. Sheridan, who was able to rub such gay elbows with the other commissars. Mr. Tchicherin's way of arching an eyebrow at life upsets the best brand of poise.

Living alone in a barren room on the top floor of the Foreign Office, he is as far removed socially and physically from the lower as the upper crust. Perhaps only an aristocrat is able to attain this dizzy height of indifference to human contact with one's fellows. And I can't help feeling that there is something rather splendid about such complete isolation.

Outside of politics, the telephone and the cable, all up-to-dateness offends him. He abhors new clothes, does not like to ride in automobiles, refuses to have modern office paraphernalia about him, does every little task for himself, like sharpening his own pencils and running all over the building on office-boy errands. This attitude produces the same effect as if he distrusted all his subordinates. His secretaries stand helpless and ill at ease while he searches for a lost telegram or answers the telephone.

Last winter they told an amusing story of how Karakhan, who is Commissar of Eastern Affairs, lured Tchicherin into donning a new suit. Tchicherin's one suit was literally in rags when the Turkish treaty and the Afghan treaty and the Persian treaty and all the other Oriental treaties were about to be signed. These affairs had to be arranged with more or less bourgeois pomp, since the Orientals are rather keen on ceremony. So Mr. Karakhan, taking a long chance, went ahead and ordered a new suit for Mr. Tchicherin from a Soviet tailor, then one morning while Tchicherin slept, he changed the suits. In a few minutes he came rushing back again and exclaimed with emotion, "There's a new note from Lord Curzon!" Tchicherin was up in one bound and struggling into the new trousers. Whatever he thought privately of Mr. Karakhan's presumption, they continued in an apparently pleasant relationship.

In appearance Mr. Tchicherin is tall, with the bent shoulders of the man who stoops to go through doors. His eyes, not through any evasiveness, but because of an extreme shyness, continually seek other places than the face of his interviewer. Yet when one meets his quick, occasional glance, one is startled by the intelligence and gentleness of his expression.

Diplomacy is an inseparable part of Mr. Tchicherin's existence. He eats, drinks and sleeps with the affairs of state, looks at life as a chess game and is continually checkmating, even in ordinary conversation. Lenin approves of him and feels for him a warm personal affection in spite of the fact that the Premier so dislikes eccentricities. He knows that Tchicherin can be trusted, that he has an invaluable knowledge of international affairs and more important than all that, that he will never make any real decision without consulting Lenin.

Mr. Bullitt told me that during his negotiations he found Tchicherin so brilliant that it was difficult to get anywhere. The Foreign Minister was always quite justified from the Soviet angle but the Soviets were being forced to make hard concessions. Invariably when they came to a deadlock, he telephoned Lenin and Lenin gave in.

During our first talk, when we discussed the campaign of lies about Russia which has so long flooded English, French and American papers, I said that I thought it was partly due to the fact that no reporters were permitted at that time to go in and investigate actual conditions. It was characteristic of Tchicherin to interrupt very suddenly and ask, "Will you tell me why American reporters come over here and claim they are impartial observers, even profess friendliness towards us, and then go home and write such astounding lies?"

I thought it wasn't fair to generalize. The most unfair stories have always been manufactured at Riga and Reval or at Paris by interested political groups or by disappointed reporters who never got inside. As for the reporters who actually witnessed the revolution, certainly the majority remained fair and sympathetic, in spite of the fact that it grew particularly difficult, especially in America, even to maintain one's equilibrium about Russia after Brest-Litovsk. To my mind came back unhappy recollections of Overman and Lusk investigations, raids, deportations and general war-hysteria. Perhaps some such thought came also to Tchicherin because he said, "Yes, yes, I suppose in the main, you are right, but how do you account for a man like——?"

TCHICHERIN

Tchicherin is full of old-fashioned honor. The idea that foreign papers sanctioned false reports in order to justify intervention or the blockade seemed so outrageous to him that he could never realize that this sort of propaganda has become as much a part of modern warfare as liquid fire or submarines.

Very late one night I saw Tchicherin running up the stairs to his office in a high state of excitement because a New York evening newspaper carried on its front page a fake interview with Lenin in which he discussed everything from the Irish situation to the Russian Ballet. Tchicherin saw no humor in this. His comment was, "How can a reputable American paper allow such a thing? After all, Comrade Lenin is the Premier of a great country."

Men who give themselves completely to an ideal quite naturally become supersensitive and unreasonable. At least that is the rule, and Tchicherin is no exception. The deliberate misinterpretation abroad, during long hard years, of every effort of the Soviet Government at peace or reconstruction or defense or negotiations, has got under his skin. So while he insisted on the strictest adherence to the truth in all reports sent over the government wire, at the same time he permitted himself a mild dissipation in extravagant adjectives by way of retaliation, in his too long and too complicated "notes." He allowed even more unrestrained language in *Vestnik*. *Vestnik* is the official bulletin of the Soviet Government—very much like the bulletin issued by the Bureau of Public Information during the war. The young man who edited this sheet was a talented and educated Russian but his idea of an unemotional government report was very much like that of our own George Creel. I used to tease him about his passion for such words as "scurrilous" in reference to capitalists or White Guards. But it never made any impression. He confessed that he found my cables flat and uninteresting.

Besides my radios to American papers, which were transmitted by way of Berlin, and the government bulletin which was sent out to the whole world and rarely used by anybody, there was also a wire to London for the *Daily Herald*. Every one of these telegrams had to be read and corrected by Tchicherin himself and I shared the unhappy fate of sitting around all night until he found time to do it. So many nights my telegrams went in the waste-basket because they contained too much American "punch" or a little "news value" or "human interest" which Tchicherin considered gossip, that for a while I regarded Tchicherin as just a fussy old man, and I almost forgot the Herculean tasks he performed in his various interlacing Eastern treaties. Or again, if one reads his correspondence with the old and settled governments of Europe, one will be startled to see how he has outclassed his adversaries. No Foreign Minister ever inherited a more difficult post and, everything considered, no Foreign Minister ever stuck to his post with more dignity and honor. It was characteristic of Tchicherin, as it is of most Russians, not to be able to strike a balance; when he did let the bars down, he let them down completely. A few months ago, we were having battles over adjectives; now reporters are given a free hand; even in Washington they do not dare criticize the government so openly. It is amusing to note that the more freedom they have the fewer harsh criticisms they find it necessary to make.

Mr. Tchicherin is a bachelor; women manifestly have no place in his dreams of a millennium. How this came to be is a secret which perhaps will never out. I am not presuming that there never was any romance in Mr. Tchicherin's life. Just

to illustrate how wrong I should be if I did, I re-
call an incident which occurred in a fashionable
Berlin café. Some Americans were discussing
Tchicherin. One remarked that she often re-
gretted that there is no room for chivalry in a
Socialist State; that equality does not recognize
gallantry. Another claimed that while Lenin
seems to have a way of treating women no better
and no worse than men, Tchicherin simply over-
looks the whole feminine sex; if he is conscious
of women at all, it is only through a slight annoyance.

Now, when the company had finally arrived at
these conclusions, they suddenly became aware of
a very aristocratic and beautiful old lady at the
next table who was regarding them disdainfully
through a gold lorgnette. Presently she exclaimed
in Russian, "How absurd you are! Mr. Tchicherin was an old sweetheart of mine." So saying,
she arose and swept grandly away, rustling in her
lavender silks, as delicate as a Dresden china doll.
So life repeats itself; there is always an Elaine
for every Launcelot. And Launcelot inevitably
deserts his lady for some vague "Light" beyond
the stars.

Tchicherin is a many-sided character. When

one sees him on the street of an afternoon blinking
and confused, with an old umbrella under his arm,
rain or shine, he appears pitiful and frail and in-
capable. . . . But if one sees him also, as I once
saw him, in an ancient, resurrected dress-suit, at
the head of a long conference table in a gold and
white hall, under glittering candelabra, speaking
in flowery and perfect French to the suave Turkish
delegates, one gets quite another idea; he appears
fine, selfless, determined.

And it is like him to admire Secretary of State
Hughes, and call him a "fine, high-minded man"
without realizing that Hughes' high-mindedness
is that of a stern, religious brother who refuses to
admit again into the family of nations the erring
and prodigal Soviet Republic; that it was Hughes
who stood out alone against the Genoa conference
until he stampeded other members of the Cabinet
and even overpowered the President. Hughes
regards Communism as immoral as Tchicherin
regards capitalism. Both men possess that unbending, cold objectiveness, that unattractive
righteousness of attitude towards those who disagree with them, which we know in America as
Puritanism. Both would have made excellent
bishops.

MIRRORS OF MOSCOW

One evening last spring I happened to be present when Tchicherin was nearly assassinated. A man flourishing a revolver appeared in the reception room and called out for the Foreign Minister. This roused a Red soldier half asleep in a comfortable chair near the door leading to Tchicherin's private office. A scuffle ensued and the soldier succeeded in getting the pistol before any harm was done.

Tchicherin refused to discuss the incident and remained obviously tranquil. He was annoyed when the Cheka tried to put extra guards at his door and absolutely balked at the suggestion that the Foreign Office be made a place difficult to enter. He simply asked every one to forget the whole incident.

I always believed that he secretly dislikes the Cheka. I remember the night that Santieri Nuorteva was arrested. It happened at midnight and was rather spectacular. Tchicherin liked Nuorteva. He was visibly upset and for a whole week he would not talk to a soul.

The confusion of the Foreign Minister's desk is a national scandal. In midwinter I have seen his summer hat still lying there, crushed under a pile of papers. I have seen papers piled high on all the chairs and sofa and gray with the dust of months. He has a fearful habit of misplacing important telegrams and then sending out a search call. Those are terrible moments in the Foreign Office. All other work stops. After everything is turned upside down some subordinate gets the courage to ask, "Comrade Tchicherin, perhaps it is on your own desk." And there it invariably is, almost on his nose, like grandmother's proverbial spectacles.

It was his habit to give a short talk about once a month to the personnel of the Foreign Office. We would meet about eight o'clock in the Foreign Office Club. Tchicherin was persistently late, sometimes one, sometimes two or even three hours. From time to time someone would whisper, "He has lost another telegram!" There would be suppressed laughter running around the room. Then suddenly the Foreign Minister would appear glancing shyly about him, clear his throat and before he began his address would explain in his high plaintive voice how sorry he was to be tardy but he had somehow misplaced a telegram. . . .

People at home have often said to me that they could not comprehend the "fascination" of the Russian revolution for an American; they have pointed out that they would find anything possible to endure except such unpleasant facts as lice and filth and lack of soap. Most of us, quite correctly, imagine ourselves capable of the larger tragedies of life and entirely lacking in the courage to face the million little miseries of an economic break-down. It is true that any man with delicate sensibilities who has stood the test of the Russian revolution has stood the test of fire. I have always believed that we are too sentimental about the romances of the Middle Ages. My opinion is that not much really that happened then was fine or good or beautiful; certainly over it all hovered no scent of the attar of roses. King Arthur's knights probably never marched away with any more noble visions before them than did those little awkward peasant boys of the Red Army. The Communists are undoubtedly the knights errant of the twentieth century and their slogan of "internationalism" is but a revival of that old, old banner of "Brotherhood." It is not altogether curious that such a whirlwind has swept into its heart a few men like Tchicherin.

In 1917, when Trotsky was Foreign Minister, I well remember a strike of his entire diplomatic corps. How it paralyzed that arm of the state! At that particular moment Tchicherin was under arrest in London. Workers with muddy boots tramped in and out of the Foreign Office with a desire to help. They were loyal to Trotsky but they were ill at ease; entirely incomprehensible to them was this intricate business of diplomacy. It is well for those same workers and peasants and soldiers that a quiet, aloof person by the name of George Tchicherin presently arrived to arrange all this business for them.

But what a paradox! Here is Mr. Tchicherin, member of one of the oldest and most aristocratic families in Russia, for four years now guiding with such delicate hands and careful brain the affairs of state, in order that all that once was, which gave his family their wealth and power, might never be again.

MAXIM LITVINOV, ASSISTANT COMMISSAR, LEONID KRASSIN AND SUBORDINATES

MAXIM LITVINOV, ASSISTANT COMMISSAR, LEONID KRASSIN AND SUBORDINATES

LITVINOV, more than Tchicherin, has been Lenin's spokesman to the outside world in the past three years. Litvinov is closer to Lenin; he knows how Lenin will react on most situations, while Tchicherin is usually in doubt. This knowledge gives Litvinov power to make immediate decisions. Litvinov has worked with Lenin since the Communist party was created, while Tchicherin actually only came into the Communist ranks after the revolution—he was formerly connected with another group and his allegiance is naturally a little more conservative.

Litvinov makes a striking contrast to Tchicherin, the aesthete. Litvinov is hale, hearty and loves the fleshy things of life. He fairly bursts with a florid, extravagant energy, like a man who has just emerged from a hot bath, dressed in haste and is late for an appointment. He is big and burly, wearing his clothes loosely with a sort of unkempt but smooth-shaven air. He is a great worker and, when he has the opportunity, a man who enjoys life greatly.

Abroad he likes to eat good food, drink old wines and roll around in a new, expensive automobile with a small red flag on the hood. All this not because he craves ease or ostentation but because of a sort of obvious patriotism for the Soviets which wants to shout to a hostile world, "We too can do things with a flourish." There is nothing subservient about Litvinov.

He has been accused of undue extravagance by the other embassies in Reval, but in Russia he goes about like any peasant with a piece of black bread in his pocket, works furiously from eleven in the forenoon until two or three in the morning to accommodate Tchicherin and never has a moment for recreation. He never looks tired and seems to begin each task with the same enthusiasm.

The Assistant Minister of Foreign Affairs is immensely human, and has an ear for jokes and gossip and knows how to hate. He has a wife and three children living in Copenhagen and maintains a perfectly conventional household. One day last winter I interviewed him while he was eating his lunch, and he said, with a sigh, that he wished he could arrange his work somehow so as to get away for a few days to visit his family. His wife had just had a baby.

"Boy or girl?" I asked.

Litvinov reddened and laughed. "The telegram didn't say," he said, "and God knows when I'll have a chance to run over and find out."

A moment later he was deep in a discussion of the attitude of the American press towards Russia. I remarked his ability to put out of mind circumstances he could not change; it is the same saving quality which keeps Litvinov from breaking under strain.

When Litvinov is interviewed his thoughts run along smoothly with no break in the thread of them; he is extremely capable and intelligent but one feels at once that he is a politician. Perhaps it would be better to say that he is a practical Communist, just as one would say that Mr. Penrose was a practical Republican and Mr. Underwood is a practical Democrat. Most successful public men are practical politicians and reporters learn early to weigh their words; they have a way of using the press, through subtle suggestions, to their own advantage.

No practical politician is above intrigue.

Tchicherin is above it and that is probably why he does not see it when it is all around him.

There was a moment when the clashing of personalities and ambitions nearly ruined the staff of Mr. Tchicherin. The whole matter centered round the English trade negotiations begun by Litvinov and David Rothstein and finished by Krassin.

Rothstein had pinned his hope on those negotiations; he believed that their successful termination would make him Ambassador to England. It is easy to comprehend his feelings and even his actions in this matter. Rothstein is ambitious without either the intelligence or the foresight of Litvinov. It is astounding that Litvinov allied himself, however briefly, in a petty intrigue against Krassin.

Rothstein has lived many years in London, his home is there, his family and his wife. No doubt it would have been very pleasant for him to have been appointed Ambassador to England. But logically, and through peculiar circumstances, that office seemed to be about to be bestowed upon Mr. Krassin. Thus Rothstein set about to remove Krassin from his path.

Both Litvinov and Rothstein had cause for deep

annoyance against the British Government. Rothstein was "allowed" to accompany Litvinov to Moscow when Litvinov was "returned" to his government; he was refused permission to go back. Feeling himself tricked, he pointed a suspicious finger at Krassin who came and went so freely. He managed to play upon Litvinov's wounded personal vanity. Between them they almost ruined Krassin's work.

Litvinov was sent out of England with all the indignity of a man being kicked down stairs. No one could blame him for a perfectly human desire to go back some day and sit at a conference table facing the very men who were once so unjust to him. This desire has probably been entirely appeased at Genoa.

The world is full of tantalizing prejudices, which direct events more than we realize. Krassin and Litvinov are both charter members of the Communist party, but Litvinov just happens to be England's idea of a Bolshevik while Krassin does not.

Because Krassin came from the same class that Lord Curzon did, England does not feel so much panic in dealing with him. Krassin is obviously a gentleman and official England can never quite ignore a gentleman. Krassin is as polished and as coldly polite and as well dressed as if he were in the House of Lords. He is tall, middle aged, fine featured and has great personal charm.

All this would not mean much in America, but in England to establish one's social equality with the home office is an especially strong point for any visiting diplomat. This acknowledgment of caste is true all over Europe. Tchicherin, the aristocrat, had a much better chance at Genoa because of his background.

If such conferences are ever held in America, Litvinov might prove the most popular of the group. Any country which is satisfied with the familiar type of our middle western Congressmen will not reject an intelligent proletarian like Litvinov. Some of our rough-and-ready Senators will surely feel much more at home with his bluntness than with Krassin's smooth, impenetrable Old Worldliness.

Litvinov reminds one of a successful mining man from Alaska or a lumber king from the West. Krassin is more like those quiet, powerful, coldly intelligent men who manage railroads, Wall Street and the world's finance.

Krassin, who once managed the great Putilov

factory and was considered one of the most able engineers in Russia, is now pretty generally conceded the strongest man next to Lenin. As a force for stability and reconstruction he is immensely valuable to the Soviets. He has maintained a mental equilibrium which many of the other Commissars have lost. Contact with men of different political opinions is a great dissolver of mental cobwebs. Krassin's continual coming and going has probably helped him to maintain his perspective. When one remains too long in Russia, the outside world often appears incomprehensible just as Russia appears incomprehensible to the outside world.

I remember a conversation I had with him during the blockade. "Whenever Russia," he said, "ceases to be a country visited only by 'brave' and 'adventuresome' and 'occasional' travelers, the Russian people and the Russian government will be no more interesting and no more evil than the governments and the people of the rest of the world; it will no longer be necessary for writers to exaggerate about us."

David Rothstein is a deep and thorough student of Socialism. Theoretically, he believes that he knows the only true way to cure the wounds of humanity; he reverences Marx as some men do Mohammed. But in real life he is fussy, narrow, selfish and without personal loyalty. He cannot imagine applying his doctrines to his immediate surroundings, and so he fundamentally fails.

Fresh from London, he spent his time ordering suits from the Soviet tailor and fuming because they did not fit perfectly; this in a country literally of rags. He was more worried about his son's dismissal from Oxford than about the thousands of young men being slaughtered on the various Russian fronts. He exclaimed generously, "We must have victory no matter how many men it takes!" But he kept his own sons in England. He could never see anything in Wells' articles for American papers except the flippant remarks about Marx which made him writhe in mental agony.

At present Rothstein is Ambassador to Persia, and Litvinov and Krassin are working in harmony.

There are many other men in the Foreign Office of interesting and varied character; very few are workmen or peasants. I will take for example, four typical men: Weinstein, Karakhan, Florinsky and Axionov.

Weinstein was one of the Editors of the Russian daily paper *Novy Mir,* in New York, and secre-

LITVINOV, KRASSIN, AND SUBORDINATES

tary to Ludwig Martens, who directed the Soviet
Bureau on Fortieth Street. He was deported with
Martens. Immediately upon his arrival in Moscow he became head of the Anglo-American
Department of the Foreign Office. Almost his
entire staff are ex-Americans. English is more
generally spoken among them than Russian.

Michael Karakhan is head of the Eastern
Department when Tchicherin is in Russia; when
Tchicherin attends the conferences, he is elevated
to Tchicherin's place. Karakhan is an Armenian
and, more through favorable circumstances than
any astonishing ability, has achieved his high
official position.

I always think of him as getting into or out of
an automobile. During the first days of the revolution he "requisitioned" Rasputin's car, a gorgeous affair which had been the gift of the Em-
press and was made especially for the mysterious
priest. Karakhan never walks anywhere and his
car is always waiting for him in front of his home
or the Foreign Office. An evidence of his clever-
ness was his ability to keep for himself the whole
lower floor of the most lovely private palace in
Moscow, while Lenin and Tchicherin lived as
meagerly as workmen.

He is a faultless dresser. And he has the rather dubious distinction of being the only Commissar who divorced his wife under the new marriage laws. He immediately married again.

Karakhan is one of those surprising figures of the revolution who, without possessing marked talents or great idealism, nevertheless rose to power.

Mr. Florinsky and Mr. Axionov represent the old order. Florinsky was a Consul in America under the Tsar. He is now a Communist and wears his red button with all the grace of an old beau wearing the ribbon of the Legion of Honor. He was the only man in Russia last year who wore spats and a monocle.

Axionov is the Cheka man—a former Tsarist officer and a poet of distinction. I was never present when he arrested anyone. He was always pounding out free verse poems between reports. Often in dull moments he read them to us.

He has the manner of a courtier and used to embarrass the American stenographers by kissing their hands. He was forever bowing and continually good-natured. Sinister rumors used to float round about his activities which caused us to vow never to "talk" or to criticize anything or anybody in his presence, but we invariably forgot our resolutions simply because he was so pleasant.

Axionov wore a beard which was fiery red. His head was absolutely bald, but he usually kept it covered by a high peaked cap with a large red star on the front. No other country but Russia could have produced such a character.

THE END